BREAKING THROUGH THE SCREEN

Practical tips for engaging learners in the online and blended classroom

Joan Kang Shin

Jered Borup

NATIONAL GEOGRAPHIC
LEARNING

Australia • Brazil • Canada • Mexico • Singapore • United Kingdom • United States

NATIONAL GEOGRAPHIC LEARNING

National Geographic Learning,
a Cengage Company

Breaking through the Screen: Practical tips for engaging learners in the online and blended classroom
Joan Kang Shin, Jered Borup

Publisher: Sherrise Roehr

Executive Editor: Laura Le Dréan

Editorial Assistant: Caroline Greaney

Director of Global Marketing: Ian Martin

Heads of Regional Marketing:

  Charlotte Ellis (Europe, Middle East, and Africa)

  Justin Kaley (Asia and Greater China)

  Irina Pereyra (Latin America)

Product Marketing Manager: Fernanda De Oliveira

Content Project Manager: Beth Houston

Senior Designer: Brenda Carmichael

Senior Art Director: Heather Marshall

Operations Support: Hayley Chwazik-Gee

Manufacturing Manager: Mary Beth Hennebury

Composition: Lumina Datamatics Ltd.

For permission to use material from this text or product, submit all requests online at **cengage.com/permissions**
Further permissions questions can be emailed to **permissionrequest@cengage.com**

Student Edition:
ISBN: 978-0-357-54185-2

National Geographic Learning
200 Pier 4 Boulevard
Boston, MA 02210
USA

Locate your local office at **international.cengage.com/region**

Visit National Geographic Learning online at **ELTNGL.com**
Visit our corporate website at **www.cengage.com**

Printed at CLDPC, USA, 02-22

Table of Contents

From the Authors

We have written *Breaking through the Screen* in response to the need for a new paradigm for both teaching and learning. This professional development (PD) book provides English-language teachers with both theory and practice for teaching effectively in online and blended learning environments. This book was inspired by a three-part webinar series we developed and delivered in March 2020, which was similarly titled: *Breaking through the Screen: Practical Tips for Engaging Learners in Online and Blended Classrooms*. This webinar series was developed in response to the global health crisis that forced teachers around the world to engage with students remotely. Not surprisingly, both teachers and students have found moving from an in-person classroom to an online learning environment challenging. Our goal in writing this book is to address those challenges and meet the needs of English teachers around the world who will continue to provide more online and blended learning options for students.

The contents of the book are both timely and on the cutting edge of education in the 21st century. *Breaking through the Screen* features 12 chapters that bridge theory and practice. Each chapter provides abundant practical ideas and examples teachers can apply to their online and blended classroom contexts. We present our ideas knowing that the tools in online teaching and learning, such as specific apps or online platforms, are ever-changing, but that the knowledge and skills teachers need will remain the same regardless of the online tools they use. We hope you will learn not only how to improve students' English-language learning online, but also how to make each student feel part of a supportive virtual learning community.

We believe the most impactful part of our book is the use of real teachers and authentic classroom applications that come from around the world. Many of the highlighted teachers are from National Geographic Learning's worldwide initiative *Learning Moments 2020*, which asked teachers to share an online teaching story—something they did in one of their classes that they wanted other teachers to know about. All of the learning moments from teachers around the world have been archived at https://eltngl.com/learningmoments/. Of the 158 entries received from 50 countries, we have incorporated 26 examples in order to show you—not just tell you—ways to develop engaging and innovative online English-language teaching (ELT). We are indebted to these courageous teachers for their exemplary work and for their willingness to share their ideas through our book to benefit other teachers worldwide.

We believe this book will be appropriate for both new and experienced English-language teachers who work with students at any age or grade level in diverse contexts around the world. With *Before You Read* and *After You Read* tasks that support teachers' understanding and application of the chapter content, this book is perfect as a PD text for in-service English-language teachers at all levels: primary, secondary, and adult. Individual teachers may purchase this book for their personal PD goals, but we also expect it to be highly useful for in-service PD programs at the school or institution level, as well as Ministry of Education-level or district-level. Teacher educators can pair this text with any ELT methodology textbook and incorporate it into their methodology courses for pre-service English-language teachers at the undergraduate and graduate level. *Breaking through the Screen* will help English teachers around the world prepare for the online and blended language learning environments that are the new norm. We sincerely hope you enjoy reading our book and begin to see yourself breaking through the screen as an innovative online and blended English-language educator!

Joan Kang Shin
Jered Borup

The authors and National Geographic Learning would like to thank all the teachers who submitted their online teaching stories to *Learning Moments 2020*. You can see their submissions at https://eltngl.com/learningmoments/.

We would like to acknowledge the following teachers, whose contributions are found in *Breaking through the Screen*.

Bandi, Monika, Romania
Bruechert, Katie, USA
Bruno, Virginia, Argentina
Cady, Kristin, USA
Cahill, Bianca, USA
Cano, Erika, Mexico
Carper, Leah, USA
Constanza, Norma, Colombia
Coutlee, Neisha, USA
Cusson, Katie, USA
Denisevich, Daniel, China
Du Preez, Stacy, South Africa
Ferrier, Halerin, USA
Gotoh, Fuiyu, Japan
Haiduchak, Katherine, Ukraine
Hashemian, Hamed, Vietnam
Hu, Xiao, China
Javes Rojas, Cynthia Evelyn, Peru
Kandaiah, Gaytri, Malaysia
Karden, Omid
Kim, Woomee, USA

Linares Lemus, Lorena Rebeca, Mexico
McLaughlin, Christine, USA
Metallinou, Anastasia, Greece
Milano, Analys, Venezuela
Monzon Torres, Odalis, Peru
Morales, Jaime, El Salvador
Murodova, Zeboniso, Tajikistan
Muslimova, Khumora, Uzbekistan
Nicastro, Ingrid, Brazil
Ortiz, Elizabeth, Ecuador
Ours, Karen, USA
Park, Esther, USA
Petit, Philippe, Mexico
Reyes Melín, Susana, Mexico
Rhaburn, Vanesha, Belize
Rojas, Scarlet, Peru
Teitsma, Corey, USA
Travaille, Caitlin, USA
Wang, Hulun, China
Yildiz, Irmak, Turkey
Živković, Ana, Serbia

CHAPTER 1
Teach Differently

"The most dangerous phrase in the language is 'We've always done it this way.'"
- GRACE MURRAY HOPPER

A student participates in an online class using her laptop at home.

Before You Read

Before you begin this chapter, think about the ways in which you integrate online technology into your English-language instruction. You might teach a fully online class or a blended class that uses both in-person and online elements. Think of the different ways you use the Internet to plan your instruction and the online software and applications you use to teach English. Also think about what types of online technology your students use to learn English. Brainstorm a list in the table below. Write the purpose for using the technology for teaching or learning as well as the advantages and disadvantages.

Name of technology (tool, software, application)	Who uses it (you, your students, or both)	For what purpose(s)	Advantages or disadvantages
Google Docs	My students	To type their writing assignments and submit them to me for feedback	Advantage: Students engage in collaborative writing and peer feedback. Disadvantage: Sometimes students delete each other's writing!

Introduction

English as a Global Language

Internet access and use have grown dramatically, and recent innovations will soon bring reliable Internet to even the most remote areas of the world. Billions of people now also use social media. This combination of easy Internet access and social media proliferation has resulted in an explosion of communication and learning.

Much of this communication is occurring in English, with over 2.3 billion speakers, including those learning English as a first or an additional language (Crystal, 2019). The British Council (2013) says of English: "As the language of communications, science, information technology, business, entertainment and diplomacy, it has increasingly become the operating system for the global conversation" (p. 5). Not only has English become the most widely used language in areas like science and technology, it is also the most widely used on the Internet (w3techs.com). At the time of publication, w3tech's analysis of known websites showed 63.6% of web content in English, with the next highest at 7% in Russian, 3.9% in Turkish, and 3.7% in Spanish. As the dominant language of the Internet, English gives people access to a wealth of information as well as direct communication with people around the world for both personal and professional purposes.

How does communication in the 21st century affect how we approach teaching English as a global language? As noted by the Partnership for 21st Century Learning, "all learners need educational experiences in school and beyond, from cradle to career, to build knowledge and skills for success in a globally and digitally interconnected world" (Battelle for Kids, 2019, p. 2). In this world where seemingly infinite information—particularly information in English—is only a click away, it isn't enough to simply integrate technology into English-language instruction. It's also important for students to develop the 4Cs: communication, collaboration, critical thinking, and creativity skills (Fig. 1.1). Without those skills, our students may learn English, but they won't necessarily be able to use it effectively in real-world digital and multimodal contexts.

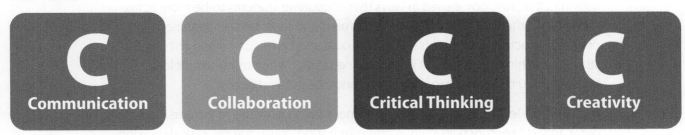

Access to technology has dramatically changed every sphere of our lives. Our world is becoming more personalized and connected. We communicate differently, we shop differently, we travel differently, we entertain differently, we form and maintain relationships differently, we work and earn differently—but do we teach differently?

Fig. 1.1
The 4Cs of 21st century skills

Why We Need to Teach Differently

Schools have a long history of telling students what to learn, how to learn, and how to show that they have learned. This one-size-fits-all approach to teaching and learning has left some students feeling disengaged and teachers feeling exhausted. Furthermore, this model is unlikely to help students to develop the communication, collaboration, critical thinking, or creativity skills they will need to find fulfilling careers.

Although teachers are increasingly using technology in their classes, there isn't any guarantee that it's improving learning. Giving students access to a laptop, for example, will not necessarily help them learn English. Technology is a tool that can have a positive impact when used well and a negative one when used poorly. Often teachers ask if technology impacts students' ability to learn English. The simple answer is "no." For instance, if a group of students reads a book in print and a similar group of students reads the same book in e-book form, their reading comprehension will be the same (Margolin et al., 2013). This is because it's the learning activity—not the technology—that impacts learning. The more nuanced response to the question of whether technology impacts learning is "Yes, if teachers use the technology to make meaningful changes to the learning activities."

Building on previous research and frameworks such as David Merrill's (2009) e[3] and Liz Kolb's (n.d.) Triple E frameworks, Borup, Graham, Short, and Shin (2021) have identified the following four goals of using technology to teach English:

- **ENABLE** Technology can unlock activities that teachers and students would not be able to do easily without it.

- **EXTEND** Technology can extend the time, place, and ways that students master learning objectives. This requires students to have access to digital scaffolding and resources anytime and anyplace.

- **ENGAGE** Technology can help increase three types of engagement—behavioral (hand), emotional (heart), and cognitive (mind). Too often students are not emotionally invested in their learning because they are given passive learning activities. If technology is used in ways that encourage students to be more active participants, they will discover more enjoyment and emotional engagement. Not only should activities be hands-on, they should also be minds-on and encourage students to think deeply about what is being taught. When using technology, teachers should try to engage students' hands, hearts, and heads.

- **ELEVATE** Technology can help to elevate learning activities to include higher-order and 21st century skills such as communication, collaboration, critical thinking, and creativity.

Elevating learning is frequently accomplished by using technology to situate learning tasks in real-world problems and projects.

These four goals of technology use, often called the 4Es (Fig. 1.2), focus on the areas most likely to impact learning outcomes. There are clearly other goals for using technology. For instance, teaching and learning take time and resources, and school administrators, teachers, and students may turn to technology to make the process more efficient and cost-effective. While improved efficiency is a worthwhile goal, focusing on efficiency alone will not directly result in significant improvement to learning outcomes because the learning activities will stay largely the same. Furthermore, it has been our experience that while technology may make specific activities more efficient, it does not necessarily make the overall learning experience more effective. However, if you focus on using technology to enable, extend, engage, and elevate student learning, you will see the real value of technology.

Fig. 1.2 **The 4Es**

Why Do You Use Technology?

Think of a recent time when you or your students used technology. What was your goal in using technology or having your students use it?

The following guiding questions can help to show how the technology impacted you and your students:

ENABLE Did the technology unlock activities that you would not be able to do easily or at all without technology?

EXTEND Did the technology provide students with flexibility in where, when, and how they learned?

ENGAGE Did the technology engage students behaviorally (hands), emotionally (hearts), and cognitively (minds)?

ELEVATE Did the technology help students to situate their learning in the real world in ways that allow them to develop higher-order and 21st century skills (e.g., communication, collaboration, critical thinking, and creativity skills)?

Improving the 4Es Using Online and Blended Learning

Over the last two decades, online and blended learning has increased in English-language teaching (Digital Learning Collaborative, 2019; Hockly & Dudeney, 2018). In some countries like China and Brazil, private language schools have been offering online English classes for students of all ages, even as young as five years old. While online course enrollments have been growing rapidly in the last 20 years, the COVID-19 outbreak dramatically increased the number of students learning online in a very short time. The number may be well over a billion worldwide or 3 out of every 4 students (UNESCO, 2020). The pandemic will likely have a long-lasting impact on learning. As Tarek Shawki, Egypt's Minister of Education, stated, "We have made more progress with digital and distance learning in the past 10 days than in the past 10 years. Without a doubt this crisis will change the way we think about the provision of education in the future" (UNESCO, 2020).

By its nature, online learning extends learning opportunities to whenever students have the time and Internet access. However, many online courses fail to fully engage students or significantly improve their learning. In fact, students are significantly less likely to pass their online courses compared to their in-person courses (Freidhoff, 2020). This is in part because often when teachers transition from an in-person environment to an online environment, they try to simply digitize what they have been doing in person. These teachers will commonly say, "I need to put my course online." This is not a good approach and may end in failure. Rather than digitizing what you've always done in person, a more effective approach is to consider the new opportunities that the technology and learning environment can afford you and your students and then design learning activities that leverage those affordances to enable new types of learning, engage students, and elevate their learning.

In addition to offering purely online courses, teachers are increasingly combining online and in-person learning. These "blended courses" allow teachers to make the most of the advantages of online and in-person teaching and may even enable them to provide students with more support than they can in in-person courses. However, if teachers aren't careful, blended courses can result in a passive learning experience that fails to leverage the transformative potential of technology.

Online and blended courses are increasing, but both require a new skill set. In fact, the skills needed to teach blended or online courses are so different from those needed to teach in person that even the best in-person teachers may not succeed in these new environments. Nervous? Don't be! We're here to help. We're going to be on this journey with you. Each of the remaining chapters of this book will provide you with ideas and examples that can improve your online and blended teaching. We only ask that you keep an open mind and be willing to try new things and—teach differently!

Teaching English Differently with Technology

Simply digitizing a learning activity may extend the activity and make it more efficient to complete, but it's unlikely to directly improve learning outcomes. Much of the technology use we observe in classrooms and in online courses is simply digitizing, distributing, and/or disseminating information. Consider how technology has been historically used in delivering a lecture. Teachers have long used technology to make lecturing more efficient. Starting with the chalkboard, teachers were able to present large amounts of information for students to passively consume. Then came the overhead projector, which allowed teachers to write on transparent sheets of plastic and project on a large screen for all students to see. This was helpful because they could reuse the transparencies year after year. Then came digital projectors, which allowed teachers to create presentations using tools such as PowerPoint or document cameras. These digital tools allowed teachers to incorporate graphics and videos in their presentations. More recently, teachers have been making video lectures that they post online for students to access.

However, what's really changed with all of this technology? Chalkboards, overhead projectors, digital projectors, document cameras, and video lectures all support passive learning. Digital projectors and document cameras are digitizing what was previously done on a chalkboard or overhead projector. Switching from a previously used technology to a new technology will not result in improved learning outcomes unless that change also significantly changes the learning activity. Richard Culatta (2013), the former director of the U.S. Department of Education's Office of Educational Technology, said in a TEDx Talk, "My fear is that if we continue on this trajectory, very soon we will have successfully replicated in digital format exactly all of the traditional teaching methods that we use today." Simply digitizing old practices or replacing older technology with newer technology will not improve our ability to teach English or prepare students for the future.

Rather than simply using new technology to replace or digitize an activity, you should seek to use technology in a way that amplifies or transforms learning activities. Royce Kimmons and his colleagues at Brigham Young University suggest that technology can **replace**, **amplify**, or **transform** ("RAT") learning activities (Kimmons, Graham, & West, 2020).

- **REPLACE** is when the teacher uses technology to digitize the learning activity or swap one technology with a similar technology without changing the core activity.
  Example: Rather than have students hand-write an essay, a teacher has their students use a word processor. The essay is largely the same, but the technology has digitized what would have been handwritten. Similarly, replacing a computer-based word processor with an online word processor will not necessarily make a meaningful change to the learning activity (unless the collaborative features are utilized in a way that amplifies the experience).

- **AMPLIFY** is when the teacher uses technology to change the activity in ways that improve teaching and learning.
  Example: Rather than have students hand-write or type an essay, the teacher has their students write blog entries. The essay is largely the same, but the technology allows students to embed images and videos and share their blog with others who can respond with comments on the blog.

- **TRANSFORM** is when the teacher uses technology to do an entirely new activity that wouldn't be possible without the technology.
  Example: Rather than type an essay or create a blog post, the teacher has their students create an edited video. Not only is the product different but so is the process that students go through to create it. In this example, students can practice the same target language (vocabulary and grammar) as in the essay but in a technology-enhanced activity (Fig. 1.3).

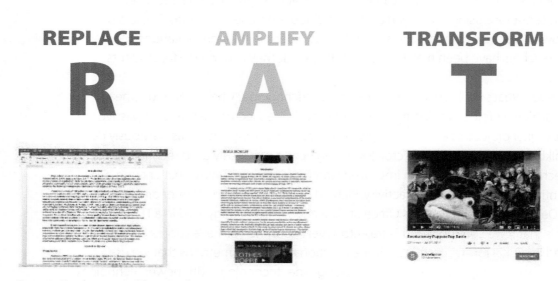

Fig. 1.3 **Replace, amplify, transform**

Kimmons et al. (2020) also categorized technology use as **passive**, **interactive**, or **creative** ("PIC").

- **PASSIVE** is when technology is used to deliver information to students but doesn't necessarily require student response or interaction. In a passive learning environment, students are watching and listening to language. They are asked to absorb and remember what is presented to them. Keep in mind that a passive activity (according to this framework) does not mean students are not doing anything! The teacher can make sure that students are listening, learning, and active in their efforts to comprehend English.
  Example: A student watches a video or attends a webinar lecture.

- **INTERACTIVE** is when students need to respond or take action. Students become active participants in the online learning environment. With language learning, it's very important to provide students with opportunities to use language. Online activities that give students a chance to interact with you and one another afford students these opportunities.
  Example: Students watch a webinar lecture and interact by making comments either verbally or in the text chatbox.

- **CREATIVE** is when students use technology to create a product. Encouraging students to use English to create a product allows them to explore new uses of language. Online technologies are making it easier for students to create products that they share with their teacher, classmates, and/or the world. Of course, depending on your students' ages and your teaching context, you might encourage students to be creative and share only with you and their peers. When students are able to share their digital products more broadly, it's important to ensure that they follow safety, citizenship, and copyright guidelines.
  Example: Students create digital presentations, infographics, digital stories, blogs, websites, edited videos—the possibilities are endless (Fig. 1.4)!

Fig. 1.4 **Passive, interactive, creative**

Now that we've learned about the PIC and the RAT, let's put them together and categorize technology use with the PIC-RAT matrix. Take a moment to look at the PIC-RAT matrix (Fig. 1.5). Starting with the vertical axis, you can see your students' technology use as passive, interactive, or creative (PIC). Along the horizontal axis, you can then see if the technology you are using replaces, amplifies, or transforms (RAT) the activities. For instance, if you use a digital projector to project slides rather than writing on the chalkboard (Replace), and then ask students to look at the slides and listen to a lecture (Passive), the activity would be categorized as PR on the matrix. In comparison, if you change an activity from writing an essay to creating a website, it would be categorized as creative and transformative (CT).

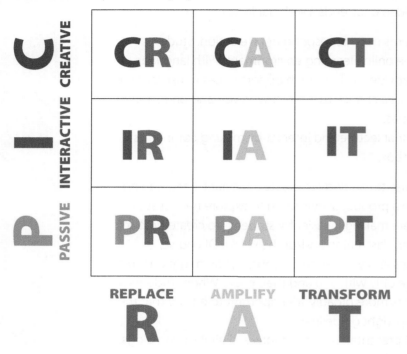

Fig. 1.5
The PIC-RAT matrix (adapted from Kimmons et al., 2020)

Application to English-Language Teaching

When teachers of English are first introduced to the PIC-RAT matrix, they tend to think that every activity should be creative and transformative (CT). While your goal may be to have students use technology to create original work, not everything that students do should be creative and transformative. Not only is that impractical; you wouldn't necessarily be providing effective instruction. Students need to have a variety of language activities from receptive (listening and reading) to productive (speaking and writing). There is a time for everything on the PIC-RAT matrix. For instance, reading an article online would be categorized as PR (passive and replace), but this is still a valuable activity. However, if the majority of learning activities are passive and don't promote interaction or production, then students won't have opportunities to use English for communication. English-language teachers should explore transformative uses of technology and discover new ways to encourage authentic uses of English.

Let's look at some examples of how to apply PIC-RAT to teaching young learners.

Read-Aloud Examples: Replace, Amplify, and Transform

Many teachers of young learners like to read aloud to help students learn language while also teaching students reading skills through modeling. Using the PIC-RAT matrix, consider how technology can replace, amplify, and transform this literacy activity, which in the PIC-RAT matrix is passive (Fig. 1.6).

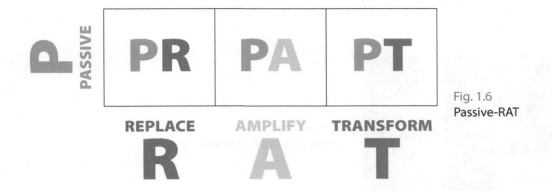

Fig. 1.6
Passive-RAT

PR (PASSIVE-REPLACE)

You can simply digitize this activity for an online course by reading aloud to students with online video conferencing tools. If you are reading a small book, you can point to the pictures or words with ease. You can also digitize the pages of a book and project on a slide. Instead of holding the book in your hands while making sure students can see you in their screens, you can share a presentation with any video conferencing software. With your hands free, you can help make input comprehensible by using gestures and the highlighter or pointer to focus students on any part of the page or text (Fig. 1.7).

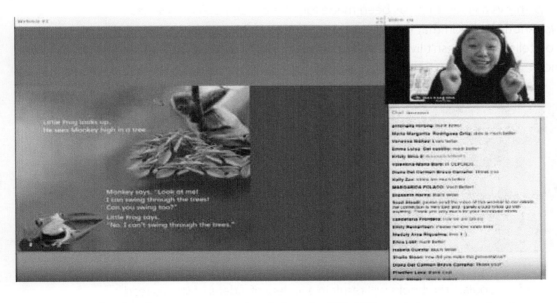

Fig. 1.7
Using a pointer to focus students on part of a page

This use of technology is an example of PR in the PIC-RAT matrix because technology simply replaced the original activity done in face-to-face environments.

PA (PASSIVE-AMPLIFY)

The same activity can be amplified (PR to PA) by giving students a recorded video of you reading aloud while holding a book or sharing a slide presentation with book pages (Fig. 1.8). If you film yourself reading aloud, students can watch the video several times to help with their comprehension. This is an amplification from the in-person read-aloud because students can rewatch and even pause the video to focus on difficult parts. In addition, you can include subtitles for learners who can read to support their comprehension with text.

Fig. 1.8
A passive-amplify (PA) activity

PT (PASSIVE-TRANSFORM)

To move from PA to PT, you can use a professionally filmed video of the story told by an actor or the author. Such videos often include multimedia effects to transform the read-aloud. This kind of video can help students with comprehension and make the story more enjoyable. Storyline Online is a popular website created by the Screen Actors Guild - American Federation of Television and Radio Artists (SAG-AFTRA) that features popular picture books in English read aloud by famous actors. They come with moving images, subtitles, and adjustable speeds, in case students want to slow down the speech. Figure 1.9 shows a video that has been made for all the storybooks in a series called *Our World*. Another option that is perhaps even more transformative is to have an author or storyteller who doesn't live locally attend your class as a guest speaker by video conference.

Fig. 1.9
Our World video,
National Geographic
Learning

A simple search for popular storybooks will result in a variety of videos of stories read aloud, some even by the authors themselves. These can be viewed by students before, during, and after any synchronous online or in-person session.

Shared Reading and Retelling Examples: Completing PIC-RAT

To continue with literacy activities, you can brainstorm ways to amplify and transform activities. Figure 1.10 shows different types of activities with technology that might be appropriate for young learners of English who are reading a particular book with the teacher. You may recognize the progression from P to I to C as one that aligns with an effective sequence of literacy activities used to replace in-person activities in an online setting.

However, even more importantly, the PIC-RAT matrix is an excellent tool to see how you can teach English differently. It provides a foundation for the concepts we will explore in this book in order to help you transform your English-language teaching in online and blended learning environments.

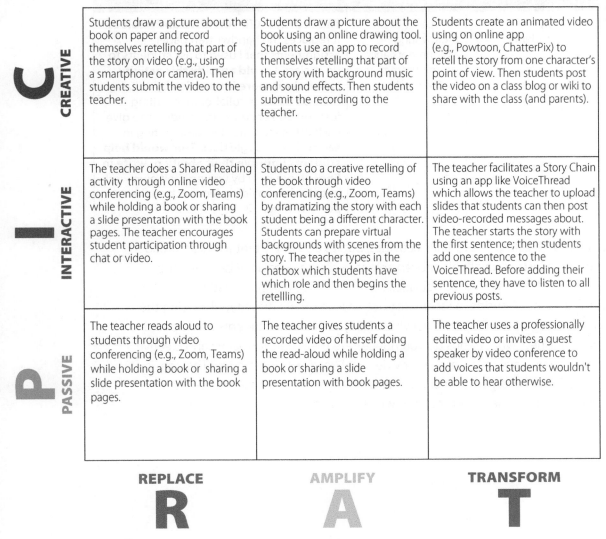

	CREATIVE		
C	Students draw a picture about the book on paper and record themselves retelling that part of the story on video (e.g., using a smartphone or camera). Then students submit the video to the teacher.	Students draw a picture about the book using an online drawing tool. Students use an app to record themselves retelling that part of the story with background music and sound effects. Then students submit the recording to the teacher.	Students create an animated video using on online app (e.g., Powtoon, ChatterPix) to retell the story from one character's point of view. Then students post the video on a class blog or wiki to share with the class (and parents).
I INTERACTIVE	The teacher does a Shared Reading activity through online video conferencing (e.g., Zoom, Teams) while holding a book or sharing a slide presentation with the book pages. The teacher encourages student participation through chat or video.	Students do a creative retelling of the book through video conferencing (e.g., Zoom, Teams) by dramatizing the story with each student being a different character. Students can prepare virtual backgrounds with scenes from the story. The teacher types in the chatbox which students have which role and then begins the retellling.	The teacher facilitates a Story Chain using an app like VoiceThread which allows the teacher to upload slides that students can then post video-recorded messages about. The teacher starts the story with the first sentence; then students add one sentence to the VoiceThread. Before adding their sentence, they have to listen to all previous posts.
P PASSIVE	The teacher reads aloud to students through video conferencing (e.g., Zoom, Teams) while holding a book or sharing a slide presentation with the book pages.	The teacher gives students a recorded video of herself doing the read-aloud while holding a book or sharing a slide presentation with book pages.	The teacher uses a professionally edited video or invites a guest speaker by video conference to add voices that students wouldn't be able to hear otherwise.
	REPLACE **R**	**AMPLIFY** **A**	**TRANSFORM** **T**

Fig. 1.10 A PIC-RAT matrix for reading activities for young learners

After You Read

Task 1: Review the activities you listed in the Before You Read section. Decide where each activity belongs in the PIC-RAT framework. Then reflect on the following questions:

- Can you amplify or transform the activity?

- Can you make the activity more interactive or creative?

- If so, how will this enhance your students' ability to use English?

Here is a sample response based on the example given above.

Name of technology	Who uses it	For what purpose(s)	Where it fits in the PIC-RAT matrix
Google Docs	My students	To type their writing assignments and submit them to me for feedback	This activity is **CR—Creative and Replace**. It replaces the handwritten paper assignments that I used to ask students to do in class. **I could amplify this activity** and **make it more interactive** by utilizing the Google Docs collaborative writing features and encouraging students to give each other feedback by commenting in each other's Google docs. **This would help students improve their ability to write in English** not only by writing their own work but also by providing feedback on their peers' writing.

Task 2: It's helpful to categorize specific activities, but it's also important to take a broader view and look at an instructional unit or even an entire course. A balance between the different types of technology-infused activities can still provide a transformative learning experience for students. Consider a recent instructional unit that you've taught. Using the PIC-RAT matrix on page 15, write in the activities that you and your students participated in. When you're finished, what trends do you notice? Are there transformative and creative uses of technology or are all/most of the activities only passive or interactive? The goal is not to have activities in every section of the matrix. Rather, the goal is to engage students in several different types of learning activities while also aiming for some creative and transformative activities.

		CREATIVE **C**	
INTERACTIVE **I**		
PASSIVE **P**		
REPLACE **R**	AMPLIFY **A**	TRANSFORM **T**

References

Battelle for Kids. (2019). Partnership for 21st century learning: Framework for 21st century learning. Retrieved from http://static.battelleforkids.org/documents/p21/P21_Framework_Brief.pdf

Borup, J., Graham, C. R., Short, C. R., & Shin, J. K. (2021). The 4Es evaluation criteria. In C. R. Graham, J. Borup, M. A. Jensen, K. T. Arnesen, & C. R. Short (Eds.), *K-12 blended teaching (Vol.2): A guide to practice within the disciplines, 2.* EdTech Books. https://edtechbooks.org/k12blended2/evaluating_bt

British Council. (2013). The English effect: The impact of English, what it's worth to the UK and why it matters to the world. British Council. https://www.britishcouncil.org/research-policy-insight/policy-reports/the-english-effect

Crystal, D. (2019). *The Cambridge encyclopedia of the English language* (3rd ed.). Cambridge University Press.

Culatta, R. (2013). *Reimagining learning* [Video]. YouTube. https://youtu.be/Z0uAuonMXrg

Digital Learning Collaborative. (2019). Snapshot 2019: A review of K-12 online, blended, and digital learning. Retrieved from https://www.digitallearningcollab.com

Freidhoff, J. R. (2020). *Michigan's K-12 virtual learning effectiveness report* 2018-19. Available from https://michiganvirtual.org/research/publications/michigans-k-12-virtual-learning-effectiveness-report-2018-19/

Hockly, N., & Dudeney, G. (2018). Current and future digital trends in ELT. *RELC Journal*, 49(2), 164–178. https://doi.org/10.1177/0033688218777318

Kimmons, R., Graham, C. R., & West, R. E. (2020). The PICRAT model for technology integration in teacher preparation. *Contemporary Issues in Technology and Teacher Education,* 20(1), 176–198.

Kolb, L. (n.d.). Triple E framework. https://www.tripleeframework.com/

Margolin, S. J., Driscoll, C., Toland, M. J., and Kegler, J. L. (2013). E-readers, computer screens, or paper: does reading comprehension change across media platforms? *Applied Cognitive Psychology*, 27(4), 512–519. https://doi.org/10.1002/acp.2930

Merrill, M. D. (2009). Finding e^3 (effective, efficient, and engaging) Instruction. *Educational Technology* 49(3), 15–26.

UNESCO. (2020, March 24). 1.37 billion students now home as COVID-19 school closures expand, ministers scale up multimedia approaches to ensure learning continuity. https://en.unesco.org/news/137-billion-students-now-home-covid-19-school-closures-expand-ministers-scale-multimedia W3Techs. (n.d.). W3Techs - World Wide Web technology surveys. https://w3techs.com

CHAPTER 2

Soar to New Heights with Assessment

"Assessment is today's means of modifying tomorrow's instruction."
- CAROL ANN TOMLINSON

GOALS

By the end of this chapter, you will be able to:

- explain the relationship between learning objectives, assessments, and activities.
- use backward design to plan assessments and activities in English-language teaching (ELT).
- use the PIC-RAT matrix to assess differently with technology and develop effective assessments for online and blended learning.

Frigate birds in flight, Galapagos Islands, Ecuador

Before You Read

Before you begin reading this chapter, let's reflect on what you already know and do related to assessment. Fill in the following table with your ideas:

- What are some examples of assessments you use with your English-language learners? Brainstorm any assessments you use. These can be in-person or online assessments.

- How and when do you assess your learners—formally, informally, every class, every lesson, at the end of a unit, or at the end of the school year?

	Formal assessment	Informal assessment
Every class	*Spelling test*	*Listening to students' pronunciation during conversations*
End of a lesson		
End of a unit		
End of the school year		

Now categorize the assessments you wrote into in-person, online, or both in-person and online assessments.

In-person	Online	Both in-person and online

Starting with Assessments

As teachers, we know that assessments are used to demonstrate how well a student has mastered the learning objectives. It doesn't matter if you are teaching English in person or online; assessments must be designed to show how well students have met the learning objectives. Often teachers think of assessments as coming at the end of a class or unit, and so they may be the last thing that they consider when designing a lesson or unit. However, assessments should be an integral part of the learning process for students and the planning process for teachers.

It's helpful to revisit some fundamental principles of assessment design. At the basic level, instructional units are made up of three things: learning objectives, assessments, and learning activities. Like the gears shown in Figure 2.1, the learning objectives work to develop the assessments, which in turn help teachers determine the activities in a lesson, which will allow students to successfully complete the assessments. Therefore, it's critical to plan assessments at the start of lesson or unit planning.

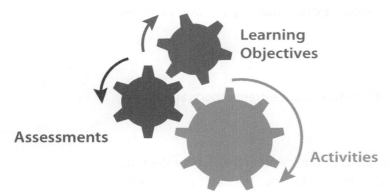

Fig. 2.1
The interdependency of learning objectives, assessments, and activities

Creating Learning Objectives

When teachers are asked to teach a course, whether in-person, online, or blended, they are commonly given a list of learning standards that they need to address. These learning standards are big-picture knowledge and skills that students should have at the end of the course. They are typically written by ministries or departments of education or more locally by committees at the school district or university. Teachers use these learning standards to create smaller unit learning objectives, which can be broken down into even smaller lesson objectives. No matter what environment you are teaching in, who your students are, or what the goal of English-language learning is, it's important to start with your learning objectives and then work backward.

When planning lessons or a unit of instruction (which consists of multiple connected lessons), it's a good idea to start by creating learning objectives based on the course standards. For English-language instruction, the following aspects of language are most often considered in learning objectives: vocabulary, grammar, language skills (listening, speaking, reading, and writing), and language functions (such as giving instructions and making suggestions). Contemporary English-language teaching (ELT) approaches focus on utilizing meaningful and relevant contexts for language learning. Therefore, when creating learning objectives, it's important to include content-focused objectives where appropriate. Content-focused objectives are those that address the real-world contexts in which the language is being learned and used. For example, university students might be learning how to find a job in English with objectives about writing a resume or doing an interview in English, or younger students might be learning about animal habitats with objectives about naming and describing where animals live.

One of the most important characteristics of a well-written objective is that it's concrete and observable. You should use action verbs that describe what students will need to demonstrate, such as *say*, *write*, or *point to*. You should avoid using verbs like *understand, know,* or *learn* because they aren't observable behaviors. Here are two well-written objectives for a lesson with action verbs that are concrete and observable:

Objective 1 (for adult learners):
By the end of the unit, students will be able to **demonstrate** their ability to do a professional job interview in English successfully **by role-playing** a realistic interview scenario with a partner.

Objective 2 (for young learners):
By the end of the unit, students will be able to **talk** about extreme sports and safety in sports.

These objectives are for assessments that are communicative and will show students' ability to use the language they have learned in meaningful ways. In Objective 1, it is clear that adult students are learning a real-life communication skill: job interviewing in English. In Objective 2, students will learn new language and content in order to talk about a youth-related topic.

Once you have written observable learning objectives, you are ready to develop your assessment. Remember that if your objective is written well, you will find it easier to create an assessment to measure student achievement of the objective. And that is your objective!

Backward Design: Starting with the End in Mind

When teaching a new course, teaching in a new learning environment, or using new modalities (i.e., online and blended), you might struggle at first to envision your instruction and assessment. We believe that it's helpful to use backward design to ensure you are assessing the learning objectives in your new environment.

Backward design, as its name denotes, is when teachers start by examining the learning objectives and designing assessments that show if students have mastered those objectives. Only after the assessments have been developed do teachers create the learning activities and provide the instructions to help students reach mastery on the assessment. Often, teachers start by creating the learning activities and only develop the assessments right before they are given. This results in assessments that may fail to measure the learning objectives because they focus on what was taught rather than on what should have been taught. Backward design, however, focuses teachers on ensuring that students master the learning objectives. Figure 2.2 shows how backward design starts from learning objectives, moves to assessment, and then finally moves to designing activities.

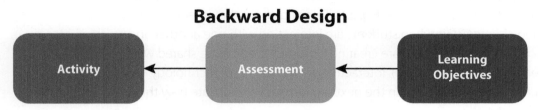

Fig. 2.2 Backward design (adapted from Wiggins & McTighe, 2005)

When teachers follow the backward design process, their learning objectives, assessments, and activities are more likely to align with each other as seen in Fink's (2003) alignment model (Fig. 2.3). Misalignment can occur in any course; however, we might see this more often when we are faced with new and unfamiliar learning environments, that is, online. Often, online students are asked to watch recorded lectures or sit in on a live lesson and then take a quiz on what they have learned. While those types of learning activities and assessments can be valuable to student learning, they typically do not align with language objectives.

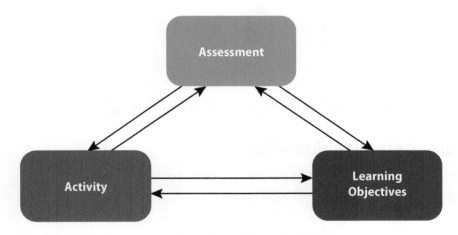

Fig. 2.3 Fink's alignment model (adapted from Fink, 2003)

Enhance Assessments with Technology

While the principles of backward design are the foundation of effective assessment design in all settings, a teacher may not feel comfortable using this process in a new and unfamiliar type of classroom, such as an online learning environment. Just remember that in an online environment, technology can be used to enhance the experience: technology can in fact make your assessments more efficient, engaging, and effective. The PIC-RAT matrix (Kimmons et al., 2020: see Chapter 1) can help you find ways to improve assessments with technology. Since all assessments require some type of student behavior or response, students are not *passive* during an assessment, and so the "passive" row has been removed from the matrix (see Fig. 2.4). Thinking about the other two rows, the use of technology is *interactive* when students are interacting with one another and/or the teacher, or *creative* when students are creating a product that can be shared with their teachers, peers, or beyond (if desired). Interactive or creative use of technology can *replace, amplify,* or *transform* assessment. In the next section, we will illustrate how this can be done in two ELT contexts.

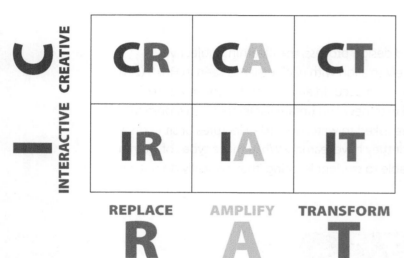

Fig. 2.4
IC-RAT model
for assessment
(adapted from Kimmons
et al., 2020)

Application to English-Language Teaching

Assessing with an Interactive Role-Play

This example is appropriate for adult learners at the university level or in business English classes. It's based on the following unit learning objective (note the action verbs in bold).

Objective: By the end of the unit, students will be able to **demonstrate** their ability to do a professional job interview in English successfully **by role-playing** a realistic interview scenario with a partner.

The culminating assessment for this unit is the professional job interview. In preparation for the interview or assessment, students are paired up and read each other's resumes and cover letters. Then they role-play both interviewer and interviewee to show they can use appropriate language to successfully play both roles. In this unit, the lesson objectives may look like this:

By the end of the unit, students will be able to:

- use strong action verbs to describe professional skills, education, and experience for a job.

- write a professional resume and cover letter for a job they want using the appropriate format.

- participate in a role-play as an interviewer and interviewee, asking and answering questions related to the job announcement, resume, and cover letter.

In a typical in-person classroom, this role-play would be prepared and practiced in pairs and then performed in front of the class. Students might dress up for the roles, and the teacher might set up a table and chairs to mimic an office setting. Let's look at ways that you could enhance this role-play using technology in an online learning environment.

REPLACE-AMPLIFY-TRANSFORM

Today, many interviews take place through an online videoconferencing tool. Furthermore, students learning English may be seeking a job internationally or in another location within their country. This means that an online interview is not only an authentic context but can also be reimagined for online and blended learning contexts.

IR (INTERACTIVE-REPLACE)

An easy replacement activity for role-playing an interview scenario would be for students to practice their role-play before class and then do the role-play in real time through a videoconferencing tool for their peers and the teacher. Depending on their proficiency in English, the students could write out a script to support their role-play or do it without a script.

IA (INTERACTIVE-AMPLIFY)

A way to amplify this interactive assessment would be to give students the opportunity to work in pairs to record the interview. They might prepare the script, memorize their interview, and make a video. The videos could be uploaded to a discussion board or a wiki in an online course management system (e.g., Canvas or Blackboard). Students could watch the videos and give their classmates feedback through text, audio, or video. Teachers could assess students' recordings and provide feedback, including a synthesis of the peer feedback as appropriate.

IT (INTERACTIVE-TRANSFORM)

In order to simulate a real-life interview, the teacher could have students work in pairs to practice being an interviewee and interviewer. The final assessment could be for students to meet individually with the teacher through videoconferencing and participate in a live interview. Alternatively, technology might enable you to invite guest speakers to interact with students in a way that might not be possible in person. If the teacher wanted to challenge students more, they could ask a job recruiter or someone who routinely conducts job interviews to come as a guest in the course through videoconferencing. This would make the interview simulation even more authentic, and the guest could answer students' questions about interview expectations.

FOCUS ON LEARNING OBJECTIVES

Figure 2.5 shows the progression of replacing, amplifying, and transforming an interactive role-play to assess students' ability to use English to do a job interview. The assessment activities have been written into learning objectives. Note that the main objective is the same in each box, which reinforces the idea that each activity will lead to students meeting the same learning objective even in an online learning environment.

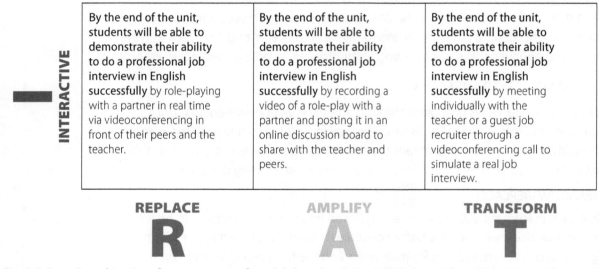

Fig. 2.5 **Learning objectives for assessments for adult learners using RAT. (adapted from Kimmons et al., 2020)**

Assessing with a Project

This example is appropriate for young learners or even teenagers. It's based on the following unit learning objective.

By the end of the unit, students will be able to talk about extreme sports and safety in sports.

This learning objective is found in a unit called "Exciting Sports" from a primary level 6 student's book. The learning objectives are expressed through "I will" statements for young learners. In a teacher's plan for the whole unit, these objectives were expressed in the following way:

By the end of this unit, students will be able to:

- talk about extreme sports.

- talk about safety in sports.

- describe people and actions.

The culminating assessment for this unit is a project, which asks students to plan an extreme sports camp (Fig. 2.6). In this project, students work in groups to brainstorm using a word web and make a brochure or a Web page. In a typical in-person class, each student would stand up and present their brochure in front of the class. Let's look at ways that you could enhance this project using technology in an online learning environment.

Fig. 2.6 **Project page from** *Our World*, National Geographic Learning

REPLACE-AMPLIFY-TRANSFORM

CR (CREATIVE-REPLACE)

A very simple example of replacing the brochure activity in an online environment would be for students to create a paper brochure and share it with the class in real time through videoconferencing. They could also take a photo of their brochure for others to view later. A replacement that would come close to amplifying would be having students create a digital brochure using word-processing or presentation software. Figure 2.7 shows an example that mirrors the hard-copy brochure. Technology makes creating a brochure more efficient and allows students to use more images than would be possible otherwise. At its core, the assessment is the same—creating a brochure with words and images.

Fig. 2.7 Digital brochure created using Google Slides

CA (CREATIVE-AMPLIFY)

To further amplify this assessment, students could use different types of technology to make the brochure interactive. They could embed videos or hyperlinks into a digital brochure. In addition, students' individual digital brochures could be posted on a class blog or Web page that would include further information and videos about various sports. This amplification would connect the project even more to real-life communication and collaboration.

CT (CREATIVE-TRANSFORM)

When you transform an assessment with technology, you need to make sure it still measures the same objectives. Figure 2.8 is a screenshot of a video created by two of Anastasia Metallinou's, students in Greece, who were 11–12 years old. Instead of creating a brochure about an extreme sports camp, they decided they wanted to create a video about an extreme sport they were particularly interested in: highlining. In this video, they describe the sport and talk about the equipment needed, the actions involved, and safety in highlining. They created a dynamic video using an online video editing program. This kind of transformative activity may require more scaffolding. In this case, the teachers helped the students by storyboarding each scene in the video (Shin, 2019). Although it was not about an extreme sports camp, this creative project was transformed into a more complex digital activity that still met the unit objectives.

Fig. 2.8 Video about highlining created by Anastasia Metallinou's students in Greece using Vyond

FOCUS ON LEARNING OBJECTIVES

Figure 2.9 shows the progression of replacing, amplifying, and transforming a creative project to assess students' ability, written as learning objectives. Like the adult example discussed earlier, the main objective is the same in each box, emphasizing that students should meet the same learning objective regardless of how the lesson is delivered or what activity they are given.

CREATIVE

By the end of the unit, students will be able to talk about extreme sports and safety in sports by creating a digital extreme sports camp brochure and presenting it to the teacher and peers online through videoconferencing.	By the end of the unit, students will be able to talk about extreme sports and safety in sports by creating an electronic extreme sports camp brochure with embedded videos or hyperlinks and posting it onto an online class blog to share.	By the end of the unit, students will be able to talk about extreme sports and safety in sports by making a video about an extreme sport they like with information to teach others how to do the sport (actions) and be safe.
REPLACE	**AMPLIFY**	**TRANSFORM**
R	**A**	**T**

Fig. 2.9 Learning objectives for creative assessments for young learners using RAT

These two examples highlight ways to assess your students when you are teaching in an online or blended environment. Technology can clearly be used to replace, amplify, and transform your assessments. The important thing to remember is that the basic principles of good assessment do not change.

After You Read

Task 1: Review the assessments you listed in the Before You Read section. Take one of your end-of-unit assessments that you would use in a typical in-person class. Decide where it belongs in the PIC-RAT framework. Then reflect on the following questions:

- Is it interactive (I) or creative (C)?

- How can you integrate technology to replace (R), amplify (A), and transform (T) the assessment? Use the following table to brainstorm activities to replace, amplify, and transform your activity using online technology.

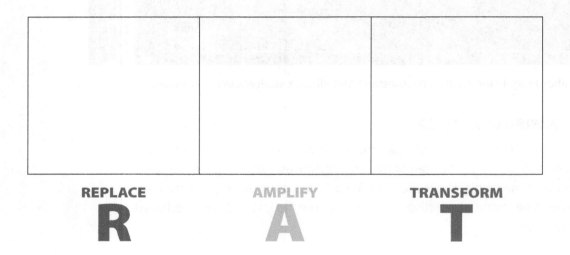

| REPLACE | AMPLIFY | TRANSFORM |
| **R** | **A** | **T** |

Task 2: Practice writing an objective and then conceptualizing it with your technology-enhanced assessments.

a. Write an objective that reflects the preceding assessment that you selected. Be sure to start the objective with "By the end of the unit, students will be able to . . .," and use an action verb that can be observed. For example:

By the end of the unit, students will be able to **demonstrate** their ability to do a professional job interview in English successfully **by role-playing** a realistic interview scenario with a partner.

By the end of the unit, students will be able to _____
_____
_____ .

b. Now write this objective in each cell of the following table, adapting it for the technology and context in which the language is being used (see Fig. 2.5 or Fig. 2.9 for an example). Each box should start with your objective and then show how your students will demonstrate the objective.

Write three objectives that align with the preceding assessments you brainstormed.

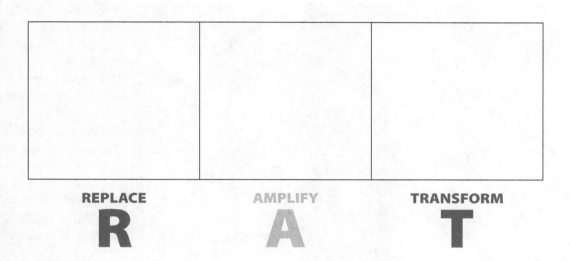

REPLACE
R

AMPLIFY
A

TRANSFORM
T

References

Fink, L. D. (2003). *Creating significant learning experiences: An integrated approach to designing college courses.* Jossey-Bass.

Kimmons, R., Graham, C. R., & West, R. E. (2020). The PICRAT model for technology integration in teacher preparation. *Contemporary Issues in Technology and Teacher Education, 20*(1), 176–198.

Shin, J. K. (2019). Use projects, and let your young learners surprise you. *InFocus Blog.* National Geographic Learning. Retrieved from https://infocus.eltngl.com/2019/06/19/use-projects-and-let-your-young-learners-surprise-you/

Wiggins, G., & McTighe, J. (2005). *Understanding by design* (2nd ed.). Association for Supervision & Curriculum Development.

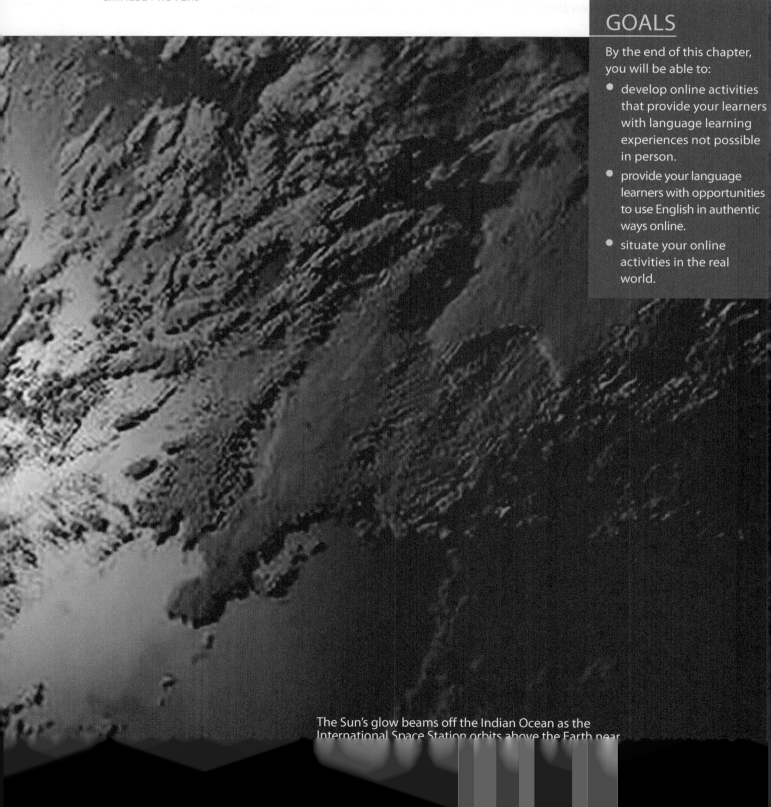

CHAPTER **3**

Bring the World to Your Online Classroom

"To learn a language is to have one more window from which to look at the world."
- CHINESE PROVERB

GOALS

By the end of this chapter, you will be able to:

- develop online activities that provide your learners with language learning experiences not possible in person.
- provide your language learners with opportunities to use English in authentic ways online.
- situate your online activities in the real world.

The Sun's glow beams off the Indian Ocean as the International Space Station orbits above the Earth near

Before You Read

Task 1: Before you begin reading, examine the learning objective(s) for your next unit or lesson. Using the backward design principles introduced in Chapter 2, decide how you plan to assess your students at the end of the unit/lesson. Think about what types of online activities your students can do that will help them complete these assessments successfully. Use the following table to write down your ideas.

Backward design brainstorming activity	
Unit objective	*Complete this sentence:* By the end of the unit, students will be able to
Unit assessment	*Describe the unit assessment that will show your students met the preceding unit objective.*
Ideas for online learning activities	*Brainstorm online learning activities that your students can do during the unit to prepare them for the unit assessment you described above.*

Task 2: Now look at the online learning activities you listed in the table in Task 1. Do these activities have real-world connections? Do they promote authentic communication in English? Underline the ones that promote authentic communication in English and think about how they can prepare your students for real-world communication.

Introduction

Technology has opened up new opportunities for English-language teaching. We know that teaching in the 21st century requires us to think differently about how we approach the English-language classroom. We live in a multimodal world where communication is not just words spoken or text on the page that we need to decode. Communication in the 21st century incorporates multimodal forms of meaning making, "with linguistic, visual, audio, gestural and spatial modes of meaning becoming increasingly integrated in everyday media and cultural practices" (Cope & Kalantzis, 2009, p. 166). It requires interpreting and producing text with images, audio, and video and learning how people use Internet technology and social media to communicate and collaborate. If we want to prepare our students for authentic communication in English, we should use a pedagogy that will engage them in contextualized language learning that incorporates these authentic multimodal, digital forms of communication (Rajendram, 2021).

As discussed in Chapter 1, the goal of online learning activities is not simply to recreate your in-person activities in the online setting. Instead, you want to leverage the power of online technology to amplify and transform learning activities in ways that improve students' language learning. Focus on what technology enables us to do, and when amplifying and transforming learning activities, focus on elevating your students' online learning experiences and incorporating 21st century skills and communication.

Promoting Authentic Communication with Social Media and Sharing Applications

While a learning management system (LMS) is an important platform for organizing and extending learning activities, there are also times when learning activities are better performed outside of an LMS using appropriate social media apps, messaging apps, or collaborative tools. These provide an excellent way to integrate the real world and build 21st century communication skills. Even better, they give students a chance to practice using English as a global language in an authentic context.

Social Media Apps

Social media apps are used daily by people of all ages worldwide. Millions of people communicate across borders in English using these apps. Teachers can incorporate social media in their English-language instruction to engage their students. For example, Cynthia Evelyn Javes Rojas in Peru engages her teenage and adult learners on her social media page where students can learn English and interact with other students around the world (Fig. 3.1). She posts tips for using English vocabulary and grammar with interesting examples, useful expressions, fun tongue twisters, riddles, and tips for living a good life. You could do something similar, using a social media app that students like to use, or encourage your students to join an existing group that you know is appropriate.

Fig. 3.1 Cynthia Evelyn Javes Rojas's Facebook page used to engage English learners

Messaging Apps

Messaging apps are a very popular way to communicate with family, friends, and colleagues. These apps can be used to send text messages, audio messages, and video messages. Many teachers use these apps to communicate with their students in English, for example, to give feedback. Teacher Vanesha Rhaburn from Belize describes how she uses a messaging app with her learners:

To keep my students motivated I send positive feedback and praise via WhatsApp. I also send them videos modeling tasks for them to try, including brain breaks and crafts that let them understand that learning is not only academic, but can foster creativity by including interactive tasks which get them moving, happy and engaged.

Analys Milano in Venezuela uses a messaging app to encourage communication that is fun and mirrors real-life daily communication (Fig. 3.2).

By creating a #Freetopic time in our WhatsApp group chat, I allowed students to share some funny images they found on internet about English use, cultural differences and ELL. For a low connectivity country like Venezuela, group chats are the best way to connect and teach online. Videocalls are difficult so instead we share images, short audios or messages. When students shared and expressed their thoughts about whatever we were mentioning, they felt heard, motivated and close to their classmates. This free topic time was a break from the "formal learning" so they would not see the chatroom as a stressful environment where all they do is homework, but instead as a virtual place where they belong and can express themselves as well.

Fig. 3.2
WhatsApp messages
between Analys
Milano's students

Having a space for students to express themselves freely without worrying about grades can be a great way to motivate them to use English for communication and build a sense of community in an online learning environment. You and your students can get to know each other socially, which can help reduce anxiety about using English as a new language. In addition, you can learn a lot about what your students are interested in via these free forums, and you can integrate those interests in your future lessons. Your students might surprise you by showing some of their personal interests and talents too!

Sharing and Collaboration Apps

There are countless apps teachers can use to promote creativity, sharing, interacting, and collaborating. These are used in the real world and can prepare students for success in higher education and professional careers. Many professors use interactive bulletin boards for students to post coursework and projects. For example, Joan Shin included a "Your Choice Activity" in her graduate course in which students could choose to create a cartoon, an infographic, a podcast, a video, or any other type of creative expression beyond a paper or essay, to show their understanding of how to motivate their culturally and linguistically diverse students to read (Fig. 3.3).

Graduate-level students can also create a digital portfolio of their work using a free Web page creation tool. As part of a professional development course, English-language teachers, like Khumora Muslimova from Uzbekistan, created digital portfolios for their reflections and examples of their teaching practices (Fig. 3.4).

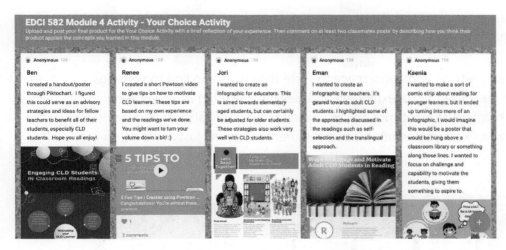

Fig. 3.3 Joan Shin's "Your Choice" activity on the interactive bulletin board Padlet for students to share their products

Fig. 3.4 Sample of Web page from Khumora Muslimova's digital portfolio

As these examples show, students at all levels can use collaborative online tools to share ideas using multimodal forms of communication that integrate images, videos, and audio recordings in addition to text. Since this is how we share content and express ourselves in real life, using these tools reflects authentic communication.

For students who are too young to have their own smartphones, messaging apps, or social media accounts, teachers can set up a private site with class-only access for them to log into through a parent-owned device. There students can practice posting texts, images, and videos. Students of all ages will benefit by learning how to use online tools interactively. After all, online communication and collaboration are important 21st century skills that all our learners need. Susana Reyes Melín in Mexico has found that using an interactive bulletin board is an excellent way to extend learning activities (Fig. 3.5).

I have adapted the use of Padlet as an online bulletin board where my students post projects related to lessons from the program. I also created a Padlet where I share songs for my students to reinforce English language.

Providing students with an additional space to share their work and find more songs to listen to/sing is a great example of extending and elevating learning activities using a popular app. Furthermore, students not only post their projects but also add reactions (e.g., thumbs up/down, like, and star ratings) and comments on them, just as we do on social media.

Fig. 3.5 Susana Reyes Melín's interactive bulletin board for sharing teacher and student content

Fuiyu Gotoh from Japan also used an interactive bulletin board as an effective way for students to share their creative work online and as a way to provide videos to introduce the topic of every lesson.

In our school, we usually have speech recital every year. Unfortunately, because of the pandemic, it couldn't happen this year. In Japan, it is very difficult to find English speaking environment for young learners. By knowing how important that English speaking output is needed, I successfully created a "Chants, Reading and Songs Collection 2020" on Padlet. Every student sent their recording to me, and I uploaded those who read and sang well as good models. It motivated those who can read or sing well. Not only the students, also the support of the parents make everything possible. They always aim high. I can feel that their reading skill has improved for those who make an effort in reading. I also posted the videos on YouTube as a gallery to introduce every topic that I used in my lessons, so that the students can recall what they have learned.

Promoting Authentic Communication with Virtual Field Trips

Field trips are powerful learning opportunities for students. Students love leaving the classroom to go to zoos, farms, or museums. Older learners can learn a lot about the real world through field trips to companies, factories, or even government offices. If you have ever taken students on a field trip, you know not only how valuable they are but also how difficult they are to organize and fund. Because of this, field trips are relatively uncommon or limited to areas within the students' immediate surroundings. While there's no substitute for in-person field trips, technology can enable more frequent and different types of virtual field trips. Using the PIC portion of the PIC-RAT framework, we can categorize students' participation in these virtual field trips as *passive*, *interactive*, or *creative*.

Passive Virtual Field Trips

You can take your students on passive virtual field trips by using videos. Videos are a great way to see places that would be difficult to see otherwise. You can use professionally made videos you find online, or you can create your own videos. Using a smartphone, you can show students various locations in their community, such as the market or government buildings. You can film yourself ordering coffee in English at a café, introducing animals at a local zoo or farm, or talking about a famous historical figure standing in front of a statue in a public square or park.

You can also use videos to take students to places that you wouldn't be able to go to otherwise. These can be far-off places or places closer to home. For instance, Katie Cusson from the U.S. filmed herself going on a ride along with a police officer as part of a unit about occupations. The video allowed her teenage students to see what a police officer does in areas of their community that were too unsafe for them to visit. They also got a close-up view of the back seat of the police car and the police station.

Interactive Virtual Field Trips

While video field trips are interesting and help students to connect with the material in new ways, it's ultimately a passive experience. You can take your students on virtual field trips at any time with virtual environments, such as Google Earth, which allows students to zoom in on satellite photos anywhere in the world. Google Earth also features Street View, which provides high-resolution, 360-degree images of streets (Fig. 3.6). With a few clicks of the mouse, students can simulate driving down the street anywhere. There are also 360-degree images called Photo Spheres, which are similar to Street View but allow you to explore areas off the road or even inside public buildings, such as the White House or national museums.

Google Arts & Culture offers students and teachers countless works of art to explore in museums around the world (Fig. 3.7). You can prepare a lesson for a virtual museum visit in the same way you would prepare a lesson for an in-person field trip. For example, you can create a scavenger hunt based on vocabulary from your lesson and encourage students to explore the museum and find everything on your scavenger hunt list. Then when you check the answers, students can describe how they found each item. Or, you could ask students to take a tour of the British Museum and find the Rosetta Stone and answer the following questions: When was it created? Who created it? Where was it found? What is it made of? How big is it? Why is it important? In this lesson, you might be teaching how to ask and answer questions in the passive voice while also teaching something new about history and languages. With these virtual museums, the possibilities for learning content and language are endless!

Fig. 3.6 **Street View using Google Earth**

Fig. 3.7 **White House virtual tour on Google**

Teachers can also make use of online maps. Jaime Morales shared how Google Maps enhances learning activities in her course (Fig. 3.8):

I am working with adults and teenagers in a Professional Forming Center. Last week, we were talking about prepositions of place, prepositions of motion, and how to get to different places. I started using a drawn map I found on the internet, but then I decided to challenge them to give the instructions using a real map of the city. So, I decided to move to Google Maps and look for New York City. The idea was that they choose a specific area to say how to get to point B from point A. At the beginning, it was just with the 2D view with not so complicated places. After practicing with some locations, I decided to move to street-view and give them the control of Google Maps to move around the city naming the streets, avenues and giving the instructions about how to move through the city to get to the place they had previously chosen.

Fig. 3.8 **Jaime Morales's Google Maps activity**

By using an interactive map with both a 2D map and Street View, students could practice giving directions while getting to know a new city. This group of students was excited to learn about New York City!

For an even more interactive and immersive experience, students and teachers are increasingly turning to virtual reality (VR) headsets. While wearing a VR headset, students can explore images, videos, or virtual environments by simply turning their heads. With VR headsets, students can virtually summit Mount Everest or dive deep into the ocean. Students can also "experience" real events, like sporting events, or fictional worlds, such as the Harry Potter themed virtual reality experiences. Premium VR headsets can cost several hundred U.S. dollars, but there are VR headsets made of cardboard that cost only a few U.S. dollars. These can be used to adapt a smartphone into a VR experience. Imagine how excited your young students would be to visit a Harry Potter theme park and be able to describe what they see using all the English they learned in your class. Or how about experiencing a deep underwater dive as part of a unit about marine conservation? These VR experiences are exciting ways to practice the language learned in class and a great way to let students experience the world.

Creative Virtual Field Trips

For a fully interactive activity, students can create their own virtual field trips for themselves, teachers, or peers. This activity can help students practice language as they develop guides and directions. For instance, students can use Google Maps to create and share maps with place markers. Within a place marker, students can add text, images, or videos. Students could create a virtual field trip of a famous city with place markers at monuments. For each place marker, students could add a description of the location, videos, and questions they would want others to answer (Fig. 3.9). As the other students went through their field trip, they could work collaboratively to answer one another's questions and even add more or edit details in the descriptions.

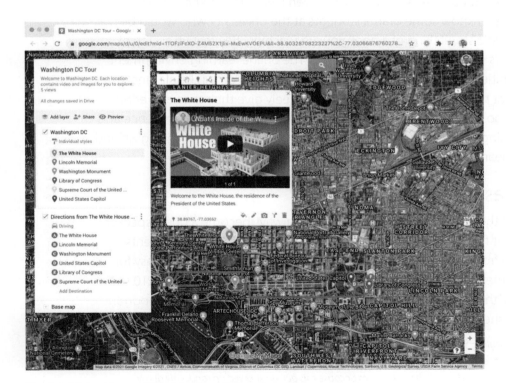

Fig. 3.9 Virtual tour of Washington, D.C., using place markers

Promoting Authentic Communication with Guest Speakers

Technology can also make it easier to bring in special guests to your class. Such guests allow for new types of interaction and promote authentic communication. In this way, not only does technology enable new experiences that might not otherwise be possible in an in-person class, it can also elevate your learning activities by situating your students' learning in the real world and providing opportunities to speak in English with real people.

Professional Guest Speakers

Technology enables you to bring guest speakers from anywhere to your class without the expense of transportation and accommodation. In a virtual environment, all you need is to find a guest speaker willing to give some time within your class schedule. You could ask the author of a book your students are reading to join a synchronous videoconference session, so that your students can ask questions. To maximize the experience, you could first help students prepare questions to ask the guest or even do a short presentation about what you learned from the author's book(s). If the time zones and schedules do not line up well, perhaps the author could send a video message for your students to answer their questions and inspire them. If you have adult students who are learning about how to conduct a business meeting in English, you could invite a business professional from an international company to give tips on facilitating a meeting. If you have young learners, you could invite a book author or a well-known storyteller to engage your students in storytelling. Even if you do not know a famous storyteller, perhaps you know some drama students at the university who would be happy to do a dramatic storytelling of a book you are teaching. Be creative and think about guest speakers who can liven up your classes. The online learning environment opens up opportunities for your students to communicate with other people, and you'd be surprised at how many people are willing to freely give their time and effort for educational purposes. Guest speakers enhance your lessons with their presence and elevate online learning activities by promoting authentic communication in English and situating students' learning in real-world communication.

The Teacher as Guest Speaker

If you can't find the right guest speaker, you could always become a guest speaker yourself! Leah Carper from the United States keeps her online high school students engaged with visits from many different "guests." Videoconferencing makes it easy for her to cover the camera and put on a costume in a matter of seconds. Figure 3.10 shows Leah dressed up as "the Grammar Grandma" to talk to her students about an important grammar point. As she explains:

> I teach 10th grade English. Something I have been doing to engage my students remotely is using guest speakers to teach concepts to my classes. The doorbell rings and someone comes to teach for a few minutes while I run an errand or call the authorities because this person showed up randomly at my

house. The guest is just me in a costume that I throw on in less than a minute. My students genuinely love it. The screenshot shows me starting a lesson about separating run-on sentences. The guest speaker is the Grammar Grandma who came to tell my students all about it. My students laughed the whole time. They engage with the guests through the chat feature. I usually have the guest stay for about 5 minutes, and then I come back (without the costume on) and pretend I don't know anything about the lesson they had with that guest speaker. Other guest speakers I had are Mr. Eddie Kit—the email etiquette expert, Detective Context—the context clues detective, and Albert Claim Esquire—the argument expert.

Fig. 3.10
Before and after pictures of Leah Carper dressed up as "the Grammar Grandma"

As Leah explains, students love interacting with these guests in this playful activity. It keeps them engaged and motivated in their online class. And having these guests is easier to manage through videoconferencing than it would be in an in-person class. This is an example of how creative use of technology for online learning experiences can engage students behaviorally, emotionally, and cognitively. Moreover, these interactions can simulate real-world communication and give students a safe and comfortable space to practice using English.

Conclusion

Technology can help you elevate your learning activities and bring the real world into your instruction like never before! Think creatively about ways the Internet can provide access to new apps and tools that can prepare your students for authentic communication that is multimodal and can build 21st century skills like communication and collaboration. The activities in this chapter are just a start!

After You Read

Think outside the box! First, make a list of your typical learning activities. You can include typical activities in an in-person traditional classroom setting as well as your online or blended class activities. If possible, make a list of online learning activities based on what you listed in the Before You Read tasks at the beginning of the chapter.

_____
_____
_____
_____

Take a look at your list. Now think outside the box. Let your ideas burst out! Write your ideas for how to create learning activities online, bringing the world to your classroom.

_____
_____
_____
_____

References

Cope, B., & Kalantzis, M. (2009). Multiliteracies: New literacies, new learning. _Pedagogies: An International Journal_, 4(3), 164–195.

Rajendram, S. (2021). A pedagogy of multiliteracies and its role in English language education. In P. Vinogradova & J. K. Shin (Eds.), _Contemporary foundations for teaching English as an additional language: Pedagogical approaches and classroom applications_ (pp. 151–159). Routledge.

Wiggins, G., & McTighe, J. (2005). _Understanding by design_ (2nd ed.). Association for Supervision & Curriculum Development.

CHAPTER 4

Create and Curate Engaging Online Content

""What we learn with pleasure we never forget."
- ALFRED MERCIER

GOALS

By the end of this chapter, you will be able to:

- use CAMEOS to evaluate and curate engaging content.
- find engaging content online.
- create your own content to engage students in online learning.
- have students generate content for online learning.

A father teaches his daughter to repair a motorcycle engine.

Before You Read

Before you begin reading, think about the kinds of materials your students find engaging. Think about your last few lessons and make a list of the content that your students found the most interesting. This is different from an activity, such as a role-play or a game. It should be content, like a reading or listening text. Complete the chart with the specific content and where it comes from.

Content your students found engaging	From textbook	Internet-sourced	Teacher-created	Student-created
Videos about farm animals	✔	✔		

Tips to Create and Curate Engaging Online Content

When teaching in an online or blended learning environment, teachers are always in search of the most engaging digital content that aligns with their course and objectives. "Engaging" means the content is enjoyable for learners based on their age as well as their personal interests. In a survey conducted in September 2020 of over 7,000 educators, of whom 75 percent had recently started teaching online, the biggest challenge reported with teaching online was motivating and engaging learners (Shin & Borup, 2021). This chapter focuses on how to create and curate engaging online content.

Additionally, for language learners, content needs to be comprehensible and presented meaningfully. After all, even the most interesting content, such as a video of your teenage students' favorite soccer player or movie star, won't keep them engaged in the lesson for very long if they can't understand anything!

As we know, engaging students online is not just finding ways to adjust our in-person teaching materials into a digital format. We have to teach differently, and this often means searching for or creating new kinds of material. As teachers, we spend much of our planning time "curating" our language teaching content. This means searching for, selecting, organizing, and preparing content to present to students. This is an important skill, and if you are new to online and blended teaching, you might find this to be your first big challenge. The good news is that as English-language teachers, we have an abundance of online content in English at our fingertips to choose from.

Evaluating Content with CAMEOS

Before we discuss different ways to curate digital content for online teaching, it is helpful to have a framework for evaluating the quality of that content. You can use the acronym CAMEOS to help you decide whether to use certain materials or how to use them for instruction. CAMEOS stands for:

Comprehensible

Age-appropriate

Meaningful

Enjoyable

Objectives

Supportive

Ask yourself these questions to be sure the digital content you are reviewing is going to be effective for your learners.

C	A	M	E	O	S
Comprehensible	**Age-appropriate**	**Meaningful**	**Enjoyable**	**Objectives**	**Supportive**
Are the language and content comprehensible for my students?	Is the content appropriate for my students' age?	Is the language presented in a meaningful context?	Is the content enjoyable and interesting for my students?	Is the content aligned with the learning objectives in my lesson?	Does the content support my students' comprehension of language?

Each element comes with some considerations for English-language teachers:

- **Comprehensible: Are the language and content comprehensible for my students?** Put yourself in your students' shoes. Will they be able to understand the language in the material? Are there samples of your target language in the material? Will they also be familiar with the cultural context and the type of information in the material? Make notes while you read, watch, or listen to the material, and write down any vocabulary or content that you think will be challenging or incomprehensible to your learners. If it is far beyond your learners' level, then you might move on to find new material.

- **Age-appropriate: Is the content appropriate for my students' age?** When you search for content online, you always have to consider if it is age-appropriate. Does it look a little childish for teenagers? Does it have inappropriate content for young learners? This is usually more important when you teach children since a lot of content online is inappropriate for kids. For example, some videos online are animated and look as if they are for children, but when you watch one from beginning to end, you may find language that is not suitable for your students.

- **Meaningful: Is the language presented in a meaningful context?** One challenge teachers face is finding good samples of authentic material that show the target language used in a meaningful context. There is a lot of content on the Internet geared specifically for language learning, but much of it focuses on decontextualized grammar and vocabulary learning. While this kind of content can be useful for certain situations, you should look for content that reflects the real world, especially if you are teaching English as a foreign language. For example, if you have a unit in your textbook about how to give advice using models, think about what real-life situations include giving advice. You could look for samples of authentic communication on a topic, for example, travel, for which you could find videos or blogs featuring a tour guide giving advice to tourists. These videos or blogs would be meaningful contexts with authentic language for presenting and practicing models of advice.

- **Enjoyable: Is the content enjoyable and interesting for my students?** When you search online, you are looking to select content that best matches your students' interests. Otherwise, you can easily lose learners' interest when teaching remotely. Find out what interests your students by asking them, perhaps via a survey of their interests. If you have young learners, you might ask their parents about what their children are interested in. This information will help you to choose appealing content for them.

- **Objectives: Is the content aligned with the learning objectives in my lesson?** While searching for the right content online, make sure you select material that aligns with your learning objectives. You should always start with your objectives so that you look for suitable content. It's often quite easy to find content that fits the C, A, M, and E, but then we forget about the O! Once you think you have found the perfect online content, go back and check to make sure it aligns with your learning objectives.

- **Supportive: Does the content support my students' comprehension of language?** Look carefully at the content you have found. Are there visuals, such as photos, illustrations, or infographics, that help make the language comprehensible? Are there subtitles or accompanying text with a video? If there is nothing to support students' comprehension, then you might consider using different materials that will help your students understand it better or creating additional materials to use with your students.

Adapting Content or Instruction Using CAMEOS

Ideally, the digital content you select has each element of CAMEOS. However, it is possible that you will sometimes have to compromise on one or more of the elements. In this case, you will want to adapt the material or your instruction to bridge any gaps. For example, you may find an article that meets your objectives and is meaningful and enjoyable, but the language is a bit difficult. It is neither fully comprehensible for your students, nor does it support their comprehension. This doesn't mean you can't use it, but it does mean you will need to scaffold the language learning in this lesson. This could include preteaching important vocabulary words, making revisions to the text to lower the language level, or using additional visual supports to aid students' comprehension. Perhaps you find a game or video that does not use your target language but is interesting and enjoyable for your students. For example, perhaps you find a great video about wild animals that matches your textbook vocabulary, but the video is in the students' language. It might still be useful since it has E and O. You can record your own translated version of the video in English as a voiceover. When you write your English translation and record the script, you know that you will have C, A, M, and S. This will ensure the content works for your students and will engage them in your language lesson.

Three Sources of Content

The content that you have to teach is often provided by your school or educational institution, yet most teachers supplement their instruction with content from other sources in order to make their language instruction as engaging as possible for their specific learners. These are three typical sources of content for your online teaching:

- Find engaging content online

- Create your own content

- Have students generate engaging content

Let's take a look at some tips for creating and curating the right content for your online classes.

Find Engaging Content Online

Like all English-language teachers, you probably already use the Internet to find content for your classes. You look for images to make vocabulary comprehensible, worksheets or interactive games for grammar practice, articles or blogs to teach reading, and videos for students to watch. Indeed, the Internet is an immense source of material for teaching, in person or virtually. The trick, however, is finding the content that will help students achieve the target learning outcomes. Let's look at an example of how to use CAMEOS when choosing videos.

FINDING THE RIGHT VIDEO

Consider a lesson for adult learners about doing an effective job interview, as we discussed in Chapter 2. The objective is:

By the end of the unit, students will be able to demonstrate their ability to do a professional job interview in English successfully by role-playing a realistic interview scenario with a partner.

The final assessment is a role-play of a job interview over a videoconferencing platform. To prepare students for the role-play, you decide to use a video that presents tips for a successful job interview. You go to a video sharing platform and search for "effective job interviews" and hundreds of videos come up. How do you decide which video to use? Use CAMEOS! First, watch the video from beginning to end and ask yourself:

- **Comprehensible: Are the language and content comprehensible for my students?**

  Most videos are targeted at proficient English speakers. If you cannot find one at the right level of proficiency for your students, search for "effective job interview esl." This may result in more comprehensible input for your students. You may, for example, find a great video that has a lot of information about job interviews that is at a level that is not comprehensible for your students but has one segment that shows the interviewer and interviewee greeting each other, which is a good illustration of appropriate body language. You can use just that clip by noting the start and end time you want your learners to view, or if you have video-editing software, you can make a clip of the part you want to use.

- **Age-appropriate: Is the content appropriate for my students' age?**

  Most of the videos will be for adult learners. However, there are some geared specifically toward teenagers. Choose one that matches your students' experience.

- **Meaningful: Is the language presented in a meaningful context?**

  You may find videos that show someone giving job interviewing tips. However, your English learners need a sample of an actual conversation. If your students have communicated that they are looking for jobs in the United States, then you might look for a video that shows a typical job interview in the United States. It should show what the interview looks like, for example, what the body language and gestures look like, as well as what to say in English. A video with these features will create a more meaningful context for your students and this particular lesson.

- **Enjoyable: Is the content enjoyable and interesting for my students?**

  After an online search, you may have found many meaningful, appropriate videos for your adult learners, but you may be concerned that they are too serious and won't really engage your learners. If you know your students respond well to humor, look for a video that is lighter or one that is a spoof of a real interview. In addition, there are a lot of "what not to do" videos for a topic like job interviews. Or perhaps you want to start your lesson with a funny video showing children answering job interview questions. Think creatively and search for videos your students will enjoy!

- **Objectives: Is the content aligned with the learning objectives in my lesson?**

  Now you need to refer back to the learning objectives. For this lesson, the learning objective is: *By the end of the unit, students will be able to demonstrate their ability to do a professional job interview in English successfully by role-playing a realistic interview scenario with a partner.* Take a look at all the videos you found. Your favorite is the funny video with kids answering job interview questions. Your students will enjoy it and certainly be engaged in your lesson. However, upon closer examination, you realize that the content in this video does not match your objectives. This funny video might have some samples of real job interview questions, but, of course, the responses are not good language models for your students to learn from. You might use the funny video as a warm-up activity for the lesson, but you still need another video that models the professional language and gestures for a real job interview.

- **Supportive: Does the content support my students' comprehension of language?**

  Ideally, you will find a video that shows what the interview looks like, including body language and gestures. The most appropriate video will show the full context of what a job interview in the United States looks like. It will explain the body language and gestures along with the language and then will show what happens in an effective job interview from beginning to end. If the video has captions, it will fully support the students' comprehension.

ADAPTING INSTRUCTION AFTER SELECTING A VIDEO

Perhaps you have selected a video that fits CAMEOS. However, you feel that your learners might still get lost in the video as they watch it on their own. Maybe your students are at different language proficiency levels, so you cannot meet "C" for all learners. You may decide to use the video anyway and adapt your instruction to provide more scaffolding for your lower-level English learners. To add further support, you might introduce key vocabulary and concepts in class before your students watch the video on their own later. In addition, you might create a graphic organizer for students to take notes on appropriate body language, gestures, facial expressions, and language. Remember to use CAMEOS as a tool for making informed decisions about how to scaffold instruction effectively as well as for finding the right online material for your learners.

Create Your Own Content

You might like to try creating your own content for class. Experienced teachers create their own content all the time. If you are new to online teaching, then perhaps you have not yet developed additional content for your course. When you create your own content to engage your learners, make sure it follows CAMEOS. There are several ways to do this.

START WITH WHAT YOU HAVE

One way to make sure that your lesson is meaningful and reflects authentic language is to develop content from your own world. When you start teaching online from home, you might feel that you don't have the school supplies or resources that you have in the classroom. Rather than focusing on what you don't have, look at the situation from another point of view. At home, you are likely to have many resources that are not at school. Consider items such as food, clothes, toys, tools, books, magazines, and even recyclable materials as resources to enhance your teaching. These are all potentially valuable treasures for your teaching that you can use to develop content that is comprehensible, age-appropriate, meaningful, and engaging. You only need to find them! Hunting for treasures in your house is as easy as 1–2–3:

Treasure Hunt

Step 1: Look at your lesson objectives.
Step 2: Go to a room in your home and look for materials to support your lesson objectives.
Step 3: Collect objects to use for your lesson.

Look through your bookshelves and even your closets. Then start by developing ideas on how to use these materials in your lesson. For example, if you are teaching how to have an effective job interview, grab professional clothing from your closets. You can use these clothes in a model video of a job interview. Your students will enjoy watching your video and will have an excellent model to follow for their role-play.

In a typical English-language course, you will likely have a unit on food. Why not look for food items in the kitchen to support comprehension of new language and make the unit more meaningful and engaging? In a synchronous (live) session, you can teach the names of fruits, such as banana, lime, apple, pear, and orange, by using real fruits from your kitchen.

USE AUTHENTIC MATERIAL

Stacy Du Preez in Port Elizabeth, South Africa, took the opportunity to create authentic material for her young learners by making a video of herself making a burger in her kitchen (Fig. 4.1). As she explains:

My students had to learn about how to make a burger. First, we learned all the ingredients and pronunciation. Then we spoke about the different steps you need to make a burger. I showed them the video to go with the lesson, and it was a real hit. The students enjoy getting a glimpse into my real life and kitchen. It makes the class more interactive, and the extra visuals make the burger activity easier to explain for such young learners.

Fig. 4.1 Stacey Du Preez's video of making a burger in her kitchen

PHOTO STORYTELLING

Integrating photos into digital materials is very easy. You can take photos of anything around the house or even look through your personal photo collections. You can use the photos to make vocabulary comprehensible and personal. For example, if you are teaching a unit on family or clothing, you can surely find or take photos on your smartphone to illustrate vocabulary. You can even collect some pictures and create a story. Fig. 4.2 is an example of Joan Shin's simple story created using photos on a smartphone. The photos and story were put into a slideshow presentation, and Joan shared her screen and told a story using these slides. It's a simple and easy way to present engaging content that fits CAMEOS!

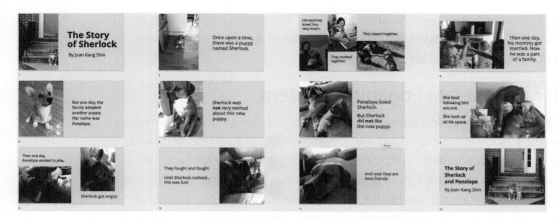

Fig. 4.2 Joan Shin's slideshow presentation of "The Story of Sherlock"

USE PHOTOS FROM YOUR OWN LIFE

Students find teacher-generated materials interesting, especially when they are connected to the teacher's life. Hulun Wang in China describes how engaged her students were with her lesson about clothes (Fig. 4.3).

I explained "Special clothes" and "Special days" by listing different clothes and dates. I let students observe, let them tell me the meaning of special. Usually, they get it right away. This is really helpful compared to you telling the students the meaning. I also shared my personal experience to explain. "People wear different clothes on different days." My students LOVE to see my wedding pictures. I am Mongolian by the way, so the clothes I wore are different and special. I shared another picture of mine to explain "Sometimes they wear clothes from the past." I shared a pic I took when I was 8 dressed up like an ancient Chinese princess. I said, "Bella wore clothes from the past, sometimes I wear clothes from the past." After viewing the pics, they now have a better understanding of the text. . . . Try the best way to get students' attention, make them realize the content is useful and meaningful, and there's a connection between content and real life.

Fig. 4.3
Hulun Wang's
"Clothes from
the Past"

Developing and creating your own materials gives your instruction a personal touch. It can even reflect parts of your life and personality, which can make your content even more engaging and exciting for your learners.

Have Students Generate Engaging Content

Another great resource for teaching online is your students. You can use student-generated content to make your lesson more personalized, relevant, and engaging. To do this, you need to think about what kinds of assignments will produce interesting student content you can use in an online setting. Think about topics and activities students will enjoy and how they can produce samples of communication to use in a future lesson. Make a specific plan for these assignments that will lead to a final product that can be used successfully in your instruction. This kind of content is especially motivating because it comes from students themselves and gives them a chance to apply new language to their own lives and experiences.

STUDENT VIDEOS

For adult learners who are learning how to have a conversation with a doctor about an ailment, you could assign them to make a video of a doctor's visit with a partner where one student role-plays the doctor and the other student role-plays the patient (Fig. 4.4). You can ask them to record their video over an online videoconferencing tool. An added advantage to this is that doctor's visits are more frequently taking place through videoconferencing, so it is an authentic way to promote this role-play.

Fig. 4.4
Sample role-play of a virtual doctor visit for adult learners

Young learners enjoy seeing each other presenting their work, and you could encourage parents to help them by making a video of their presentations to share with the class. Figure 4.5 shows a student presenting his project through a video that a parent recorded.

Be sure you let students know in advance that you will select the best videos to use in the next lesson. In the synchronous session, you could select one model video and facilitate a discussion about how the video best reflects the assignment. Or in an asynchronous class, you could have students post their videos in a discussion board and ask them to provide peer feedback. Student-generated videos are an excellent source of engaging content for learners.

Fig. 4.5
Student presentation
recorded by a parent

ONLINE SHOW AND TELL

In a Show and Tell activity, students show one of their belongings, usually a favorite toy or object, and tell the class something about it. Teachers can assign a Show and Tell based on the lesson. For a synchronous session, you might have students show their own objects during the class so that you can help them with vocabulary and check their comprehension. If you are teaching colors, you could assign students to find three things that are blue and bring them to class. If you are teaching about food, ask students to find and bring one fruit and one vegetable. If you want to check their comprehension of clothing, ask students to bring examples of a shirt, pants, socks, and shoes to show you. Fuiyu Gotoh from Japan was teaching a unit on toys and asked students to grab their favorite toy and do a Show and Tell. In Figure 4.6, you can see a boy holding up and presenting his Buzz Lightyear toy with some models of language to talk about toys in the learning platform. As Fuiyu explains:

After learning the grammar, I give them a few minutes to bring their favorite toys and use the grammar to make sentences of their own. They enjoy very much sharing their favorite toys with each other. They can't bring their toys or dolls from home to the classroom, but they can share online from home. "Favorite" is very difficult for Japanese to pronounce. I found that after this engaging online activity, most of them got familiar with this word!

Fig. 4.6 Fuiyu Gotoh's students' Show and Tell using a classroom presentation tool

This type of activity can work with teenagers and adults too. If you have a unit with teens focused on pop music, you could have some students do an Audio Show and Tell by asking them to post their favorite song on your learning management system. Perhaps you are teaching adults a unit about hobbies. You could give them a chance to share something that represents their hobby, such as bread they baked, a sweater they knitted, a trophy from a sports competition they won, or photos from a hiking trip (Fig. 4.7). There are many opportunities for students of all ages to do a Show and Tell about something in English.

My hobby is hiking with my son. This is Acadia National Park, Maine, U.S.A.

Fig. 4.7 **An adult learner presenting her hobby**

STUDENT PROJECTS

Another excellent source of course content is student-generated projects. Why not use the excellent work your students have created in class? Not only does it give students a sense of pride and an authentic purpose for their project, but it also gives the class a chance to appreciate each other's work. Xiao Hu in Zhengzhou, China, had students create their own menus as part of a unit on eating out at restaurants (Fig. 4.8).

This activity is an opportunity for students to explore their own interests by creating their own menu. Students are encouraged to create a menu based on the photos of menus provided by me and their own research and share their thoughts on what a menu should look like by adding their own design. They are encouraged to put real life dishes on their menus or put any made up ones they choose to. . . . Often students research the food and other cultural aspects of their menu selection. . . . This activity also encourages students to put a price for each dish. Doing so helps students understand the value of money. It also allows them to think about the world through firsthand experience by using the menus they created to act out scenes like "order in a restaurant." . . . Some classes will have a real-life experience at an outdoor section of the class to visit a restaurant (one with an English menu) and order their own food. This way they could really relate what they learned to the real world, so they would have a better understanding of it.

Fig. 4.8
Xiao Hu's students' menus

In this creative blended activity, some students were able to go to their pretend outdoor restaurant with the menus they made and order food. In a 100 percent online learning environment, the teacher could share students' menus through videoconferencing and use them to practice the language for ordering food. Either way, students can practice real-world language. What an exciting and engaging way to learn English!

Using student-generated work to teach English ensures that your content follows CAMEOS. Make a clear plan for yourself when you want to use student-generated content. It's important to give your students clear instructions for how the content should be created and how you are going to use it afterward. If students complete your assignment well, then it should fit CAMEOS! Creating content can be enjoyable for your learners because they are adding a part of themselves to your instruction and can share their good work with their peers.

Finding engaging content that is just right for your students is not always easy, but hopefully these tips will help you create and curate comprehensible, age-appropriate, meaningful, enjoyable, and well-scaffolded digital content that aligns with your course and objectives. Using CAMEOS will help you plan effective lessons to engage your students in online and blended learning environments.

After You Read

Task 1: Search the Internet for an engaging reading or video. Now analyze this material to see if it fits CAMEOS.

Title of reading or video: _____		Yes/No	Notes (why or why not?)
C	Are the language and content comprehensible for my students?		
A	Is the content appropriate for my students' age?		
M	Is the language presented in a meaningful context?		
E	Is the content enjoyable and interesting for my students?		
O	Is the content aligned with the learning objectives in my lesson?		.
S	Does the content support my students' comprehension of language?		

Reflection: Based on your analysis, will you use this content? Why or why not? If you are missing one of these elements but still want to use the content, what can you plan in your instruction to ensure your students will get the most out of this resource? For example, if you found the perfect video for your lesson that your students will love, but it is a bit too difficult for their language level (i.e., missing C but has AMEOS), how can you scaffold the language input to make sure it is comprehensible to your students?

Task 2: Pick an upcoming lesson and brainstorm different types of engaging content that you might choose to use. Use the following graphic organizer to guide your brainstorm.

Lesson title: **Lesson objective(s):** By the end of the unit, students will be able to . . .	
Based on your lesson objectives, brainstorm the different types of content you can use for this lesson by searching and selecting, developing and reading, and assigning and utilizing.	
FIND ENGAGING CONTENT ONLINE	
CREATE YOUR OWN CONTENT	
HAVE STUDENTS GENERATE ENGAGING CONTENT	

Reference

Shin, J. K., & Borup, J. (2021, March 25). *What have we learned about teaching during the pandemic?* [Presentation]. 55th Annual TESOL Convention, Virtual.

CHAPTER 5

Be Crystal Clear

"In an effective classroom, students should not only know what they are doing, they should also know why and how."
- HARRY WONG

GOALS

By the end of this chapter, you will be able to:

- write clear instructions for online learning activities.
- use technology effectively to make instructions clear to your students.
- recognize the importance of an organized online learning environment.
- prepare a variety of activities to orient your students to learning online.

A sign on a trail going to the Lewis and Clark Caverns, Montana, USA

Before You Read

Before you begin reading this chapter, think about your online learning environment and the instructions you give your students. Reflect on the following questions:

Reflection questions	Answers
1. How do my students know where to go or log in for learning activities?	
2. How do my students know what to do for each learning activity?	
3. How do my students know when assignments are due?	
4. How do my students know what my expectations are for attendance, activities, participation, assignments, and assessments?	
5. How often are my students confused about what they're supposed to do in the online learning environment? How do I know they are confused?	

Reflection: Based on your answers, do you think that the instructions you give your students are crystal clear?

The Importance of Being Crystal Clear

We recently asked a teacher experienced in both online and in-person teaching what advice she would give to teachers who are new to online teaching. Without hesitation, she said, "Make sure you have clear expectations and directions. That's the biggest difference between teaching online and teaching in person—you have to be crystal clear online."

It's not that clear directions aren't important in person—they are! However, when you are with your students in person, they can ask for clarification and you can quickly respond. Even if your students aren't verbally asking for clarification, you may see confusion on their faces and be able to intervene on the spot.

On the other hand, when you are giving directions online, it can be difficult to read the room and recognize student confusion. In an online or blended teaching environment, participants can't always rely on the visual cues typically found in a classroom. Monitoring students directly, as you would in a classroom, becomes challenging at a distance. Opportunities to circulate and "drop in" are limited. Furthermore, students may be completing learning activities asynchronously or without your real-time presence. In these cases, it takes students longer to get clarification if they have questions. At times, you may not even know that your students were confused until they start submitting work that is far from what you were envisioning.

And so, in the world of online and blended teaching, clarity is more important than ever. No matter how effective your activities and assessments are, if directions are unclear, they will not benefit your students. Unclear expectations and directions can leave online students feeling frustrated and isolated.

Giving Clear Directions

Back-to-back drawing is an activity that highlights the difficulty of both giving and following directions. In this activity, two people sit back-to-back. Person A holds a simple drawing and describes the drawing to Person B. Person B listens and draws the picture on a sheet of paper, without looking at the original drawing. If you've ever engaged in this activity, you know it can be challenging. The results are often hilarious! The picture Person B draws rarely looks exactly like the picture that Person A described. Not surprisingly, some people are better at giving directions than others, and some people are better at taking directions than others. Whenever you give directions, it's important to remember that some students may be learning to do the task for the first time and don't have the same vision for what needs to be done. We are more likely to provide clear directions when we put ourselves in our students' shoes and consider all of the information that they require.

Despite the challenges inherent in not being with your students in a classroom, there are actually some advantages to giving and receiving directions online. Most teachers know that live directions are often insufficient: even if your directions are crystal clear, students who are distracted will need to have directions repeated. And even when students are paying attention, they can benefit from receiving directions in a way that allows them to go at their own pace. Online directions are on-demand, and this ensures that you won't have to repeat directions over and over.

Let's look at steps to making online directions crystal clear.

Steps to Giving Clear Directions

- **Step 1: Clearly describe what students will be creating. If possible, display a model.** Are they creating a poster, a dialogue, a role-play, or a paragraph? It's helpful for students to be able to see models of what they will be creating. When possible, use examples previously created by other students.

- **Step 2: Break complicated tasks down into smaller, specific steps.** When students are asked to do complicated projects, it's important that you break them down into smaller, more manageable tasks or steps.

- **Step 3: Provide visuals.** While you can give directions with text only, some information is better conveyed with images and/or videos. That's why physical models are so helpful.

An example of Steps 1–3 can be seen in the project "*My World* Circles" (Fig. 5.1). Notice that:

1) there's a clear description of what students are expected to do,
2) the project has been broken down into smaller steps, and
3) each step is illustrated clearly for students to follow. An example of the final product is also included.

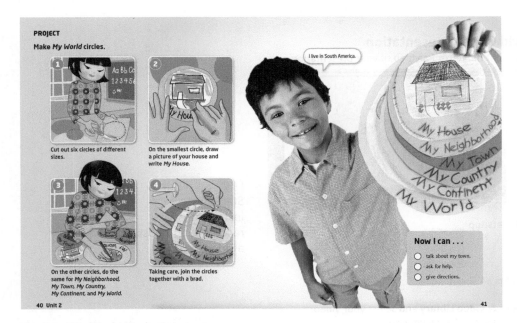

Fig. 5.1 "*My World* Circles" project

- **Step 4: Share an assessment rubric early.** In Chapter 6, "Focus on Feedback," we recommend using assessment rubrics to more efficiently provide students with feedback. If you create rubrics early and share them with students *before* they begin an assignment, they'll know exactly what they need to do and what they will be graded on. Figure 5.2 shows an example of the rubric for the project "*My World* Circles."

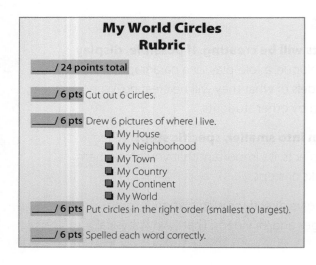

My World Circles Rubric

_____ / 24 points total

_____ / **6 pts** Cut out 6 circles.

_____ / **6 pts** Drew 6 pictures of where I live.
- ☐ My House
- ☐ My Neighborhood
- ☐ My Town
- ☐ My Country
- ☐ My Continent
- ☐ My World

_____ / **6 pts** Put circles in the right order (smallest to largest).

_____ / **6 pts** Spelled each word correctly.

Fig. 5.2
Rubric for a project

- **Step 5: Provide technology support.** When the assignment requires the use of technology that is unfamiliar to students or is outside of the learning management system (LMS) platform you are using, it's important to provide additional support. Figure 5.3 shows instructions for students (and parents) for posting a video presentation in a WhatsApp class group. Because this is outside of the school LMS, the teacher provided step-by-step instructions on how to post a video recorded on a smartphone.

My World Circles Presentation
1. Use your phone. Record a video of your presentation.

2. Open WhatsApp

3. Go to **Class #4** Group Chat.
4. Tap +
5. Tap **Photo & Video Library** and select your video.
6. In "Add a caption…" type your name.
7. Tap ▶
8. Done!

Fig. 5.3
Step-by-step instructions for recording and posting a video

- **Step 6: Consider how instructions can be misinterpreted, and then make modifications.** Once you've finished drafting directions, read them over as if you were a student. Try to anticipate any questions or misinterpretations that students may have. If necessary, make modifications so that the directions are completely clear.

Using Visuals, Video, and Think Alouds to Give Clear Directions

VISUALS

Providing visuals (Step 3) is especially important when students are asked to complete complex tasks. The Media Richness theory (Daft & Lengel, 1984) suggests that some media are better than others at conveying complex information. Daft and Lengel explain that text alone has low richness, and while it is possible to convey a lot of information in text, it may confuse a student if it is complex, as is the case with many assignment directions.

Teachers can increase the richness of the information by adding images, audio, and video recordings to directions. Consider the experience many of us have had when we purchase something that requires assembly. If the assembly directions are text-only, they can be confusing. Having an image of what the final product looks like and images showing what to do for each step is extremely helpful.

VIDEO

At times, even images are not enough, and it may be necessary to provide video directions. A quick video explaining a rubric can help focus students on your expectations for an assignment. Students can rewatch the video to review expectations if anything seems unclear at first.

Perhaps the easiest way to create visual directions for digital assessments or tasks is to perform the task yourself on your computer. As you do the task, record your screen, using a screen-recording tool. When selecting a tool, pay attention to limits such as how long the video can be, or the number of videos you can create for free.

Screen-recorded directions are especially helpful when the task is to be completed on a computer. If the task isn't meant to be completed on a computer, you can film yourself with your smartphone as you complete the model manually. Figure 5.4 shows screen grabs and the teacher script from a short video that was created to explain a rubric to students before they began working on writing a product review.

We've gone over what a product review is. And we've looked at this model. We've underlined the parts that make this a good product review—the places where you give your opinion of the product.

> **WRITING**
>
> When we write a product review, we describe a product. We give examples of what's good and what's bad about it. We can use adjectives to help the reader understand our opinions.

33 Read the model. Work in pairs to find the good and bad points about the product. Underline the good points. Circle the bad points.

Do you like the smell of cookies baking? Fresh flowers? Well, it's now possible to experience these great smells electronically. You just need a cool new gadget for sending smells, scent pellets, and an app on your smartphone or tablet.

This product is amazing because it lets you send smells to people anywhere in the world. Sharing smells can help us connect to an idea or an experience better than just looking at a photo or reading a text. Think about it: you're making cookies. You take a photo of the cookies using the app. Then you tag the photo with certain smells, like chocolate or butter. You can combine tags to create more than 300,000 different smells! I love how the product lets you be creative in mixing different scents. I also like the idea of receiving smells. So, if my friends are camping and I'm not there, at least I can smell the burning campfire!

This product is incredible, but there are some things about it that I don't like. First, the gadget is big and not very mobile. It would be great to receive smells wherever I go. The company is working on this problem. They're creating bracelets and smartphone cases that will let users receive smells, but these products aren't available yet. The product is also pretty expensive. It may be a while before a lot of people have them, so there won't be many people to share smells with. All in all, I give this product three out of five stars!

34 Discuss in pairs. Would you like to try this product? Why or why not?

35 Write. Write a paragraph to review a product that you have used. Explain what you like and don't like about it. Use adjectives to help your readers understand your opinion.

People can send scents by tagging photos, and receive them using this tabletop device.

123

Now, I'm going to introduce you to the rubric. This looks like rubrics we've used before. Notice the number system with 4 being Excellent, 3—Good, 2—Needs improvement, and 1—Redo.

Writing Rubric
Use this rubric to assess students' writing. You can add other aspects of their writing you'd like to assess at the bottom of the rubric.

4 = Excellent
3 = Good
2 = Needs improvement
1 = Redo

	1	2	3	4
Writing Ideas are clear and well organized.				
Grammar Student uses *will* and *going to* to talk about the future.				
Vocabulary Student uses a variety of word choices, including words used in this unit.				

Fig. 5.4 **Video directions** (*Continued*)

But notice that I have added an extra line at the bottom for the requirements of a product review. You need to give your opinion of the product, give examples of what's good and bad, *and* use appropriate adjectives to describe what's good and bad.	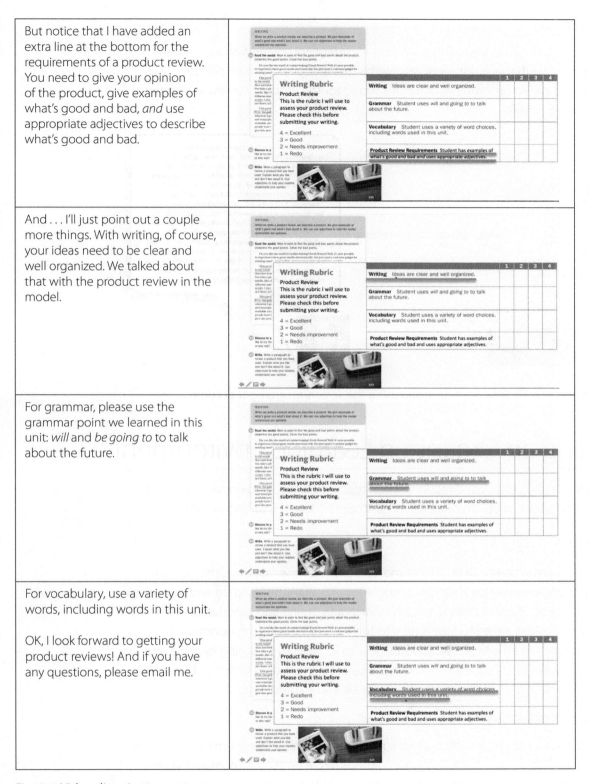
And . . . I'll just point out a couple more things. With writing, of course, your ideas need to be clear and well organized. We talked about that with the product review in the model.	
For grammar, please use the grammar point we learned in this unit: *will* and *be going to* to talk about the future.	
For vocabulary, use a variety of words, including words in this unit. OK, I look forward to getting your product reviews! And if you have any questions, please email me.	

Fig. 5.4 **Video directions**

THINK ALOUDS

During a Think Aloud, you role-play being a student completing an assignment. As you work through the assignment, you verbalize what you are thinking, step by step. Figure 5.5 shows an example of a Think Aloud for the Product Review assignment discussed in Figure 5.4.

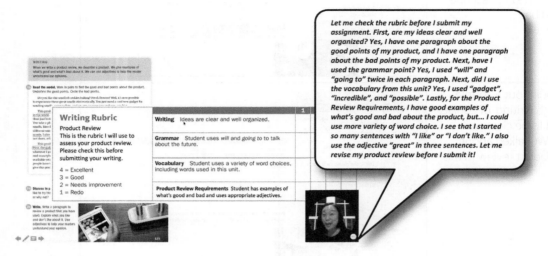

Fig. 5.5 **Example of a Think Aloud recorded using the screen-recording tool Loom**

Creating an Organized Learning Environment

In addition to giving clear directions when teaching online or blended courses, it's equally important to create an organized and student-friendly learning environment.

Orienting

When students come to a brick-and-mortar school for the first time, they usually attend an open house where they can become familiar with the building and meet their teachers. This type of orientation is just as important in online and blended courses and even more important if the student is new to this kind of learning environment. You will need to take the time to show students how to log into the learning systems and programs they will be using. You will also need to allow them time to get to know and explore their online learning environment. Here are some useful tips:

MAKE SHORT SCREEN-RECORDING VIDEOS

If students are new to an online platform such as an LMS, show them how to log in and navigate the platform. A good way to do this is to create screen-recording videos. Shortly before the start of the course, send your students a short video showing them how to log into the course. Once they're in the course, you can send them another video that shows how to navigate it.

OPEN YOUR COURSE EARLY

If possible, open up your course a week or two early. Invite your students to look around and get acquainted with the course. If you've already sent a video with instructions for how to log into the course, your students will have time to explore, make mistakes, and learn how to navigate the course before the learning begins. This type of preparation can help students feel more comfortable and confident about using the LMS platform.

DO A SCAVENGER HUNT

A scavenger hunt that instructs students to answer questions about information in their course and syllabus is a fun way to introduce your students to the course. The hunt can also require students to perform tasks that they may need to perform during the course. For instance, ask students to find your email address in the course syllabus and send you an email with a subject, a greeting, and a question regarding the course. At the end of a designated time, you can have students submit their completed scavenger hunts for grading, another task that they'll need to perform during the course.

START WITH PRACTICE ACTIVITIES

Imagine how stressed students can be if they have an important assignment that's worth 20 percent of their grade, but they're not sure how to submit it. We recommend giving students time to practice using the features of a new platform with a low-stakes activity before they use the platform for graded learning activities. If you ask students to submit assignments through a specific assignment link, try to make the first submission an activity that isn't worth a lot, or even *any*, points.

Figure 5.6 shows a page in an LMS designed specifically for submitting assignments. The first assignment due is a Student Profile Form that isn't worth any points but does give students an opportunity to practice using the assignment feature. If a student is unable to submit the assignment successfully, the teacher can help them work it out before the next assignment, which may be graded.

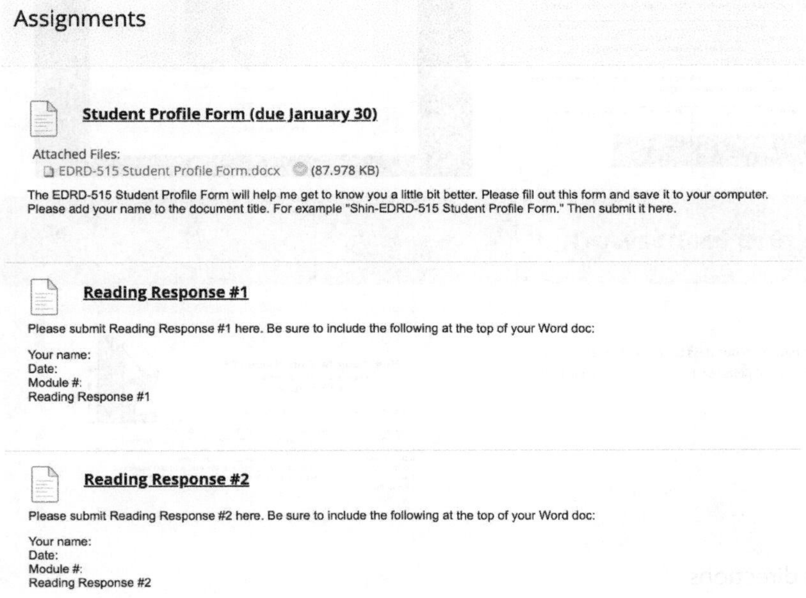

Assignments

Student Profile Form (due January 30)

Attached Files:
EDRD-515 Student Profile Form.docx (87.978 KB)

The EDRD-515 Student Profile Form will help me get to know you a little bit better. Please fill out this form and save it to your computer. Please add your name to the document title. For example "Shin-EDRD-515 Student Profile Form." Then submit it here.

Reading Response #1

Please submit Reading Response #1 here. Be sure to include the following at the top of your Word doc:

Your name:
Date:
Module #:
Reading Response #1

Reading Response #2

Please submit Reading Response #2 here. Be sure to include the following at the top of your Word doc:

Your name:
Date:
Module #:
Reading Response #2

Fig. 5.6
An LMS page for submitting assignments

SET COURSE EXPECTATIONS

In addition to orienting students to the platform and tools, you should orient students to instructional units or specific assignments. Whether you're in an in-person environment or meeting your students online in real time, take a few minutes to preview what students will be learning and doing during the class and to offer support. When you're not meeting in real time, a combination of text and short video recordings that clearly highlight learning objectives, assignments, and other course expectations can serve as a preview of the unit.

Tips for Providing Clear Organization and Directions

Regardless of whether you're using an LMS, a website, or a combination of different platforms, it's up to you to provide clear organization and directions. There's no one-size-fits-all formula, but there are general guidelines that you should try to follow.

CHUNK DIRECTIONS AND CONTENT

It can be intimidating for students to see a long page of directions and material, so it's better to chunk that information into different sections with heads, bullets, and graphic elements, or even on separate pages. You can use blank space and headings to chunk the content on a single page. Figure 5.7 models how clear headings and a little blank space can do an effective job of breaking up content.

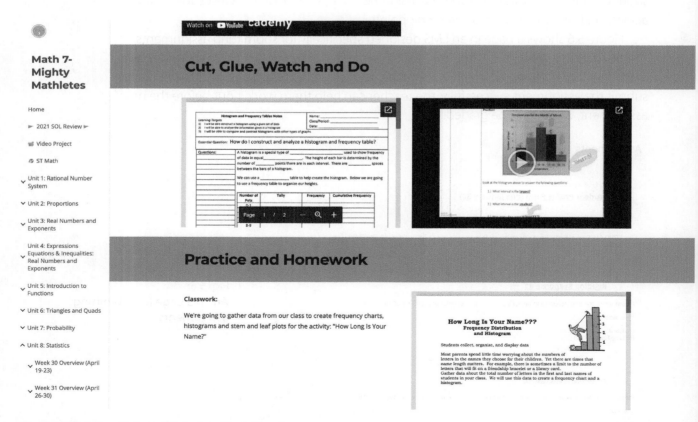

Fig. 5.7 Christine McLaughlin's chunking directions

USE BULLET POINTS, NUMBERED LISTS, AND BOLD TYPE

Bullet points or numbering can make it easier for students to read and follow steps or lists. When information is long or complex, it's best to start with a bold summary. Bold keywords within a text can also help to focus students' attention.

LEFT-JUSTIFY PARAGRAPH TEXT

When text is centered, it can be difficult for students to read because it's a little harder to find where a sentence continues. It's generally better to left-justify all text, but center the main headings.

SHORTEN THE LINE LENGTH

When text extends all the way across the screen, it can take longer to read because your eye has to cover more ground going from the right of the page to the left. Developing readers may also accidentally skip lines when their eyes have to travel all the way across a screen.

USE SYMBOLS AND ICONS PURPOSEFULLY

Icons can be used throughout a course to signify certain tasks or activities. For instance, Karen Ours, a primary school teacher, uses the icons shown in Figure 5.8 to cue students for what is provided or asked in class.

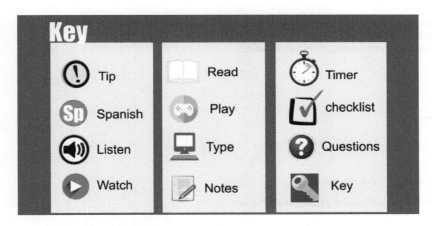

Fig. 5.8 **Karen Ours's student cue icons**

EMBED VIDEOS

Rather than linking to external videos, embed videos directly into the page unless they are optional. Figure 5.7 shows an embedded video.

USE CLEAR AND SIMPLE FONTS

English-language students may still be learning how to read the English alphabet. Stylized fonts that make letters look unusual can look cool, but they may make it more difficult for English students to read a text. Use simple fonts like Arial, Helvetica, or Calibri that show letters in their standard form.

AVOID SMALL TEXT

Text should be at least 12-point or larger, especially if you have younger students. It is much easier to read and causes less strain for the eyes.

ENSURE THAT THERE IS A SENSE OF FLOW IN YOUR COURSE NAVIGATION

You don't want students to feel lost in the online learning environment or not know what to do next, so check that your course navigation makes sense.

Using Checklists to Provide Reminders

It can be helpful to provide students with checklists that contain all of the activities they're expected to complete. Checklists don't provide students with the directions they need to complete assignments and tasks, but they do make it less likely that students will accidentally skip a task or assignment or turn assignments in late. Some checklists can be included at the end of a module within your LMS as a reminder to students to make sure they did everything in the module. It can be helpful to write them using simple "I" statements in the past tense, such as "I watched three videos" (Fig. 5.9), so students can easily see whether they completed everything.

Module 1: Wrap-up

This is the end of Module 1! I hope this was a good introduction to TEYL. I am sure you learned a lot about the characteristics of young learners and how children learn. Look at the checklist below, and make sure you completed all of the assignments for this week.

Checklist:

☐ I watched three videos.

☐ I read two articles.

☐ I took a quiz.

☐ I posted 2 (or more) messages in the discussion.

☐ I submitted my assignment called " Learning Environment Profile"

In Module 2, you will learn about classroom management. Now that you know about the characteristics of young learners, you can apply this knowledge to managing the classroom. Get ready for another exciting module!

Fig. 5.9 **Checklist at the end of a module in the Canvas LMS**

Checklists can also be easily created in a word-processing document with a two-column table, with the activity listed in one column and an area for students to check off the task in the adjacent column. Figure 5.10 shows a two-column checklist for students to make sure they have completed everything in a multi-lesson unit on how to write an opinion.

You'll know you're done with Lessons 9–12 when you can check off all the items in the table.

Activity Name	Mark an "x" when you finish the activity.
With your group, complete Opinion I Lesson.	
With your group, complete Opinion I task.	
With your group, complete Reasons Lesson.	
With your group, complete Reasons Brainstorming Planner.	
With your group, complete Examples Lesson.	
With your group, complete Examples task.	
With your group, complete Opinion II Lesson.	
With your group, complete Opinion II task.	
Turn in your OREO Method Playlist for credit.	
Complete this table and turn in this assignment in Google Classroom.	

Fig. 5.10
Checklist for assignments in a multi-lesson unit

You can customize your checklists depending on your specific class. Some classes will be at different proficiency levels or have different needs or goals. You might have required as well as optional activities to help guide learners, or you may wish to include extra exercises for students who need more practice. Be sure to make it clear which activities are required and which are optional. In the checklist in Figure 5.11, the required items are bold and are labeled "R".

Check the items off as you complete them. Make sure you complete all **required items (R).**

Orientation	
Complete the Entry Writing Assessment (R).	☐
Review the orientation instructions and videos (R).	☐
Complete the Orientation Quiz (R).	☐
Lesson 1	
View the presentation "What is Good Writing in English?" (R).	☐
Read "What's my reader's point of view?"	☐
Complete the ranking activity based on "Qualities of Powerful Writing."	☐
Lesson 2	
View the presentation "Overview of Verb Tenses" (R).	☐
Review the handout "Verb Tenses Chart" (R).	☐
Read "Preparing to Write" and "Common Irregular Verb List."	☐
Lesson 3	
View the presentation "Present Tenses" (R).	☐
Complete the workbook practice pages and check your answers.	☐
Discussion Board	
Post your introduction in the Discussion Board (R).	☐
Reply to the posts of others in the Discussion Board (R).	☐

Fig. 5.11
Checklist showing required and optional assignments

After You Read

Task 1: Think about two or three times your students were confused about where to log in or what to do next. Then answer the questions in the following table.

Examples of when my students were confused in my online or blended class	What instructions or supports did I give my students when they were confused?	What new strategies can I use to make my instructions crystal clear?

Task 2: Look at your online course, and choose a set of directions for a complex, multi-step activity. It could be a project, a writing assignment, or an activity using an app that is outside of your LMS platform.

Write down the instructions here or copy and paste them into a blank document. Use the tips and suggestions from this chapter to make your instructions crystal clear!

Step 1: Write down your instructions. These should be your existing or current directions.

Step 2: Revise your written instructions based on the tips in this chapter.

Step 3: Add other supports for your instructions to make your directions crystal clear.

Reference

Daft, R. L., & Lengel, R. H. (1984). Information richness: A new approach to managerial behavior and organizational design. In B. M. Staw & L. L. Cummings (Eds.), *Research in organizational behavior* (Vol. 6, pp. 191–233). JAI Press.

CHAPTER 6
Focus on Feedback

"There is no failure. Only feedback."
- ROBERT ALLEN

Friends give each other feedback on photos.

Before You Read

Before you begin reading this chapter, think about how you provide feedback to students. Fill out these checklists to see how you approach giving feedback. *(Check all that apply.)*

When I teach in person, I give my students feedback . . .	When I teach online, I give my students feedback . . .
❏ at the end of a unit.	❏ at the end of a unit.
❏ in every class.	❏ in every class.
❏ on every assignment.	❏ on every assignment.
❏ by correcting their mistakes.	❏ by correcting their mistakes.
❏ by praising them for correct answers.	❏ by praising them for correct answers.
❏ by praising them for an answer (correct or not).	❏ by praising them for an answer (correct or not).
❏ with a letter or number grade.	❏ with a letter or number grade.
❏ with a description of how to improve.	❏ with a description of how to improve.
❏ by using a rubric.	❏ by using a rubric.

Look at your checklist and reflect on your answers. Are there differences between your answers for in-person and online teaching? When you teach online, what are the challenges for giving feedback that differ from those for your in-person classes? What are some advantages?

Giving feedback in online settings	
Challenges	Advantages

The Importance of Feedback

Feedback is a critical part of teaching and learning. Feedback is different from regular instruction because "feedback is a 'consequence' of performance" (Hattie, 2008, p. 174). However, in learning environments that place a premium on providing feedback, instruction and feedback can become intertwined. As teachers, we need to carefully assess students' performance and provide them with quality feedback that will increase their likelihood of success.

In his groundbreaking synthesis of over 800 meta-analyses focused on student achievement, John Hattie, director of the Melbourne Education Research Institute at the University of Melbourne, found that feedback is correlated to student performance. However, some types of feedback are more helpful than others. Instead of simply working to increase the *quantity* of feedback, teachers should first focus their efforts on improving the *quality* of the feedback that they provide. When we are teaching in online and blended learning settings, the teaching environment affects how we provide feedback and how it is received. In this chapter, we will first discuss what constitutes quality feedback. We will then share models and strategies for providing quality feedback online.

What Is Quality Feedback?

Considering the amount of time that teachers spend providing feedback, there is not as much research as you might expect about what makes quality feedback. As one researcher said, "We need more feedback on feedback" (Eraut, 2006, p. 118). However, research does suggest that feedback should be (1) specific, (2) kind, and (3) timely.

SPECIFIC　　　KIND　　　TIMELY

1. **Specific:** Quality feedback is specific and personalized to the student's performance. Not only does feedback need to describe the strengths and weaknesses of students' work, but it should provide students with the information and assistance to close the gap between their performance and the established criteria for success.
2. **Kind:** Students are most likely to apply their feedback when it is delivered in a positive, encouraging, and respectful manner (Gikandi, Morrow, & Davis, 2011). The tone and delivery of feedback may depend on the age of the learner as well as the context of the classroom (Short, Becker, Cloud, Hellman, & Levine, 2018). However, kind feedback is especially important at the start of the course when students tend to be somewhat insecure in their ability to succeed and communicate in English. Giving feedback that is perceived as kind and respectful is also a valuable opportunity to form or strengthen teacher–student relationships.

3. **Timely:** The content of the feedback is only important if it is provided to students when it's still useful. As a rule, the sooner after a student's performance, the better. That said, the type of assessment and student performance can determine the amount of time it takes to provide feedback. When there is going to be a delay between students' performance and feedback, it's best to tell students when they should expect to receive the feedback.

If any of these three attributes is missing, the feedback is less likely to impact learning. For instance, teachers can provide students with timely and kind feedback, quickly providing them with generic comments such as "Great work!," but those types of comments are not specific or personalized to a student's performance and are unlikely to have a meaningful impact on learning. Additionally, if students feel that the feedback delivery is unkind, it can harm important relationships, leaving students unmotivated to improve their work regardless of how specific the comments were or how quickly the feedback was provided. Finally, feedback can be specific and kind, but it's unlikely to be used by students if it's not provided in a timely manner. Figure 6.1 shows how quality feedback has all three attributes.

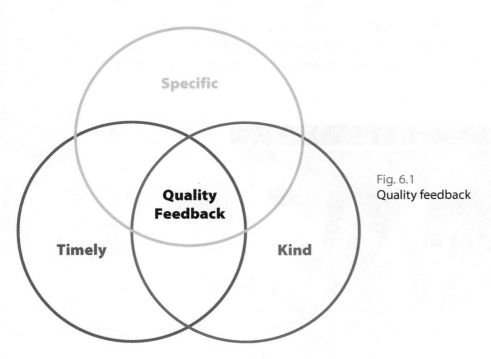

Fig. 6.1
Quality feedback

In addition to these three characteristics of good feedback, it's also important to consider the focus of the activity. If the purpose of an activity is communication in English with a focus on meaning and fluency rather than accuracy, then teachers should avoid corrective feedback and consider feedback based on meaning. For example, if you are checking comprehension of a story or video, it's best not to interrupt a student's answer even if they make grammatical or pronunciation mistakes. Instead, better feedback is given right after the student answers your question (timely) and involves asking a question for clarification (kind and specific).

Providing Feedback Online

As the PIC model demonstrates, online learning activities can be passive, interactive, or creative. By definition, feedback comes as a result of student behavior, so teachers can only provide feedback during or following interactive or creative activities.

For instance, when teachers are communicating with students synchronously such as during a videoconference, they can provide students with feedback during the regular flow of the lesson as seen in the following exchange about the video shown in Figure 6.2:

> *Teacher: Class, what were the elephants doing in the video? Raise your hand if you have an answer.*
> *Students: (Clicking on hand icon in videoconference)*
> *Teacher: (Unmute Jina) Jina, what were the elephants doing in the video?*
> *Jina: Elephants playing soccer.*
> *Teacher: Yes, the elephants were playing soccer. What else were they doing?*
> *Jina: The elephants were running.*
> *Teacher: Excellent. What else were the elephants doing? Look at the chatbox for your sentence starter. Raise your hand if you have a sentence.*

In this example, the teacher didn't use explicit correction, such as *"That was wrong. You need* were *before playing. The* elephants *were* playing soccer!*"* The teacher focused on meaning. However, the feedback was still timely, kind, and specific enough that it did elicit a more grammatical response.

Fig. 6.2 "Elephants playing soccer" video discussed with students in a chatbox

In online and blended learning, when you use creative learning activities that your students complete over time, it's important to consider how that will change the ways you provide feedback. For these types of activities, students often need more time than you have in synchronous classes, whether online or in person, to prepare or complete a project. The submission and/or presentation of these types of products usually requires different kinds of feedback. Unlike in the preceding interactive example that is happening in real time, when students take the time to create something to demonstrate their learning, you may need to take time to carefully consider students' performance before providing feedback. When you teach online or in a blended environment, you can provide students with feedback messages using text, audio, or video. Each has advantages and disadvantages.

Text-Based Feedback Messages

Most online communication is text-based. Teachers commonly provide students with text comments via email, or in notes attached to students' work. They do this within an online gradebook or with a grading rubric. Providing feedback via text has two clear advantages. First, students can read the feedback quickly and easily refer back to what was written. Second, text feedback is easy to give. However, relying on text feedback has some disadvantages. First, because it lacks many of the communication cues present in video or in-person communication, it is more prone to being misinterpreted. For instance, when a teacher provides critical feedback using text, the student may mistakenly believe that the teacher is upset. This is especially true if the student hasn't previously formed a friendly relationship with the teacher— something that can be difficult to do using only text communication. Furthermore, if a student has a lower level of English proficiency, they may not understand modals or other grammatical constructions used to soften constructive feedback or make suggestions. A teacher might not want to write "This is wrong" which, although clear to a beginning student, would be rather harsh in tone. The teacher might write instead, "It would be better to write it like this." With the more tactful written feedback that uses the conditional, the student may not realize what is wrong. Therefore, it's helpful to have other types of nonverbal cues to ensure the feedback is kind, clear, and not demotivating.

Another disadvantage of providing feedback by text is that typing detailed feedback comments can be time-consuming. Teachers can make the process more efficient by creating a comment bank with frequently used statements that can be copied and pasted into feedback comments. Rubrics can also help to efficiently convey text feedback. Digital rubrics are a common grading tool in learning management systems. Typically, a rubric lists the grading categories in the left column(s). The columns to the right—often three or four columns—then describe different levels of mastery for each category. Figure 6.3 shows a rubric for participation in a university-level online discussion.

Total possible points = Quantity of posts + Quality of posts		
0–10pts Reflects 0–3 posts with various levels of quality	6pts Posted 3 messages of required length	4pts Posts reflect high level of critical analysis of course unit content and of others' ideas. Posts made contributions that incorporated new perspectives on course content and others' ideas to further the discussion.
		3pts Posts reflect some analysis of course unit content and of others' ideas. Posts made valid contributions to group discussions.
	4pts Posted 2 messages of required length	2pts Posts reflected analysis of course unit content, but did not reflect analysis of others' ideas.
	2pts Posted 1 message of required length	1pt Posts did not reflect analysis of course unit content, but reflected some analysis of others' ideas.
	0pts Posted no messages of required length	0 points Posts did not reflect analysis of course unit content or others' ideas.

Fig. 6.3 Rubric for participation in a university-level online discussion

Another way of using a feedback rubric is for the teacher to describe the criteria and then check adjacent boxes to indicate the degree to which the criteria were met. Figure 6.4 shows an example of this style of rubric. Note that, the ratings (1–4) are defined in the key.

Writing Rubric

4 = Excellent
3 = Good
2 = Needs improvement
1 = Redo

	4	3	2	1
Organization Ideas are clear and well organized.				
Grammar Student uses correct grammar.				
Vocabulary Student uses a variety of word choices, including words learned in this unit.				
Writing type Student describes events in a person's life. Student uses words such as *after (that), before, since then, the next year, then, at the time, suddenly,* and *afterward* to clearly connect events.				
Usage Quotation marks are used correctly.				
Others _____				

Fig. 6.4 Sample writing rubric

Figure 6.4 is a rubric from a young learner series. This rubric can be easily embedded in an online course assessment system. Most learning management systems have rubric generators that you can customize with your own point system and standards. These also include comment boxes, so you can provide personalized feedback beyond checking off the generic descriptions. Using these comment boxes can reduce the impersonal nature of rubrics, ensuring that students receive more personalized and specific feedback.

Audio and Video Feedback Messages

Online tools are making it easier to give feedback using audio and video recordings. If you search for free audio recording tools online, you will find several tools that allow you to quickly record your voice. Once you have recorded your message, you will get a link to the recording that you can share with your students.

Similarly, there are a growing number of free online screen-recording tools that allow you to easily record anything on your computer screen. You can add audio narration to make your feedback friendlier, more specific, and clearer.

These online screen-recording tools primarily allow three types of recordings: webcam only, screen recording only, and screen recording with webcam.

1. **Webcam-only** videos are especially helpful when you want to form friendly relationships. Students can see you and your facial expressions and feel a stronger connection to you. These visual cues can also be helpful to avoid miscommunication. Webcam video feedback can be especially helpful at the start of the semester when students are still forming a relationship with the teacher (Fig. 6.5).

Fig. 6.5
Webcam-only video

2. **Screen recording only** videos are helpful when you need to show and comment on specific aspects of a student's work. Since you can record anything on your screen while recording your voice, you can simply pull up students' digital projects (e.g., videos, blogs, website, and infographics) on your computer screen and then use your cursor to circle or highlight specific parts of the video while describing them (Fig. 6.6).

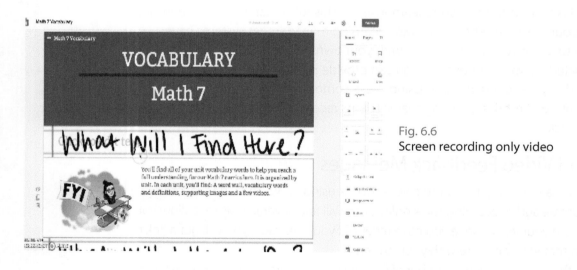

Fig. 6.6
Screen recording only video

3. **Screen recording with webcam** videos combines the best of both worlds by allowing you to share your computer screen, give oral feedback, and show a webcam video of you talking. Some tools will also allow you to alternate between showing the screen recording and the webcam (Fig. 6.7).

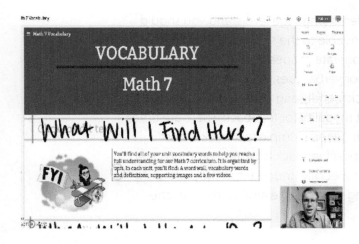

Fig. 6.7
Screen recording with webcam video

Research has found that students generally appreciate the video feedback that they receive from teachers (Borup, West, & Thomas, 2015). Students tend to find the feedback more friendly and specific than text feedback. However, there are some drawbacks to providing and receiving video and audio feedback. First, when compared to text feedback, providing audio and video comments can be harder and more time-consuming because the feedback needs to be recorded in a relatively quiet place. Teachers who are new to providing audio and video feedback may feel the need to rerecord videos when they make small mistakes in their speaking. It can be frustrating when you rerecord a feedback comment multiple times in an attempt to get it "just right." Students can also find video and audio feedback less convenient than text because it's more difficult to refer back to specific parts of the recording while they are revising their work. Despite these drawbacks, students find video feedback comments more detailed, personalized, and kind compared to text feedback.

Here are some strategies for making video feedback more efficient and effective:

1. **Be natural.** Resist the urge to rerecord messages after small mistakes or pauses. When we speak in person, it's only natural to have imperfections. In text, it's easy to remove those little mistakes, but video is time-consuming to edit and we do not recommend even trying. When recording video, it's more important that you speak naturally. Students actually appreciate those small imperfections because it humanizes the teacher.

2. **Be prepared.** Before recording your video message, it's good to know generally what you want to say. We don't recommend writing a script since using a script reduces the authenticity of the message and can make it feel robotic. You may want to type up brief notes to remind you of what you want to say. These notes can also be provided to students with the video comments.

3. **Be personable.** Remember that the student will be watching the video, so speak as if the student was actually there with you. Remember to smile and look into the webcam to create a sense of eye contact, and speak with energy.

4. **Be comprehensible.** You know your students' language levels, and you should remember to make your speech understandable to the student who is watching the video. If you need to slow down your rate of speech, try to make sure it still sounds natural and authentic. Using nonverbal cues, like gestures and facial expressions, will help to make the feedback friendly and comprehensible.

5. **Be strategic.** Video is not always the best modality for feedback. There are times when text feedback is easier and better. In general, simple feedback is best communicated using text and more complex feedback is better communicated in audio or video. Video feedback can be especially important at the start of the semester when students are still becoming comfortable around their teacher.

Example of Video Feedback

In Chapter 2, you saw an example of a video students produced about an extreme sport—highlining. This was an example of an assessment that was creative and transformed from the original brochure about an extreme sport camp. Two students worked together to create a video, and the teacher provided video feedback by playing the students' video and recording a screencast of her reaction to it (Fig. 6.8). Notice that the teacher stopped the video after each scene and gave feedback that was personable and comprehensible. Although the teacher did not have a script, she did prepare some thoughts by watching the video once before.

Teacher feedback	Video narration	Screenshots from video feedback (recorded using Loom)
	Highlining. By Amalia and Christiana	
	Highlining is an extreme sport. People walk across the rope tens of meters above the ground or the water.	

Fig. 6.8 Feedback on student video (*Continued*)

Teacher feedback	Video narration	Screenshots from video feedback (recorded using Loom)
Great introduction. You're speaking nice and clearly. And, I really like your choice of extreme sport: highlining. I don't know very much about it, so I can't wait to learn some more. Here we go!		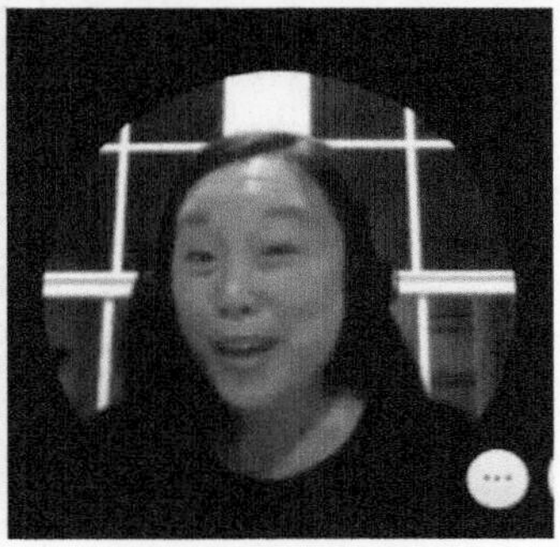
	People can do it all year round. In winter. In spring. In summer. And in autumn.	
	Highlining is a very dangerous sport and only people with experience and many skills can do it.	
	To do it you need: a mainline of webbing, backup webbing, and either climbing or armsteel rope.	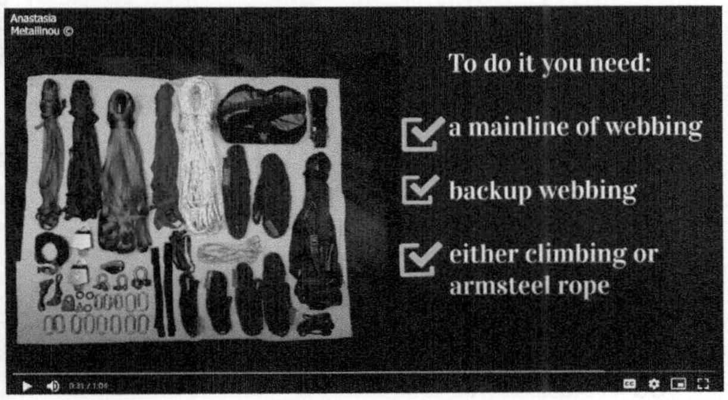

Fig. 6.8 **Feedback on student video** (*Continued*)

Teacher feedback	Video narration	Screenshots from video feedback (recorded using Loom)
OK, it does look dangerous. And you definitely need to know what you're doing to go highlining. I don't know what the webbing is or what armsteel rope is exactly. So it could be helpful in your video if you have an arrow pointing to each one when you read the list.		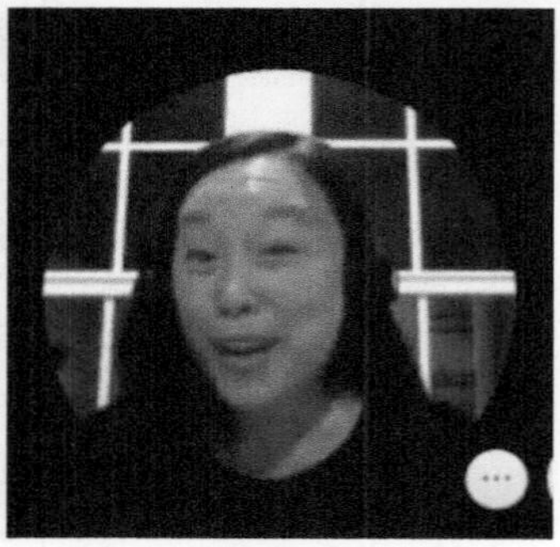
	Now one joke: If you fall, then the only way to survive is . . . (drumroll sound effect).	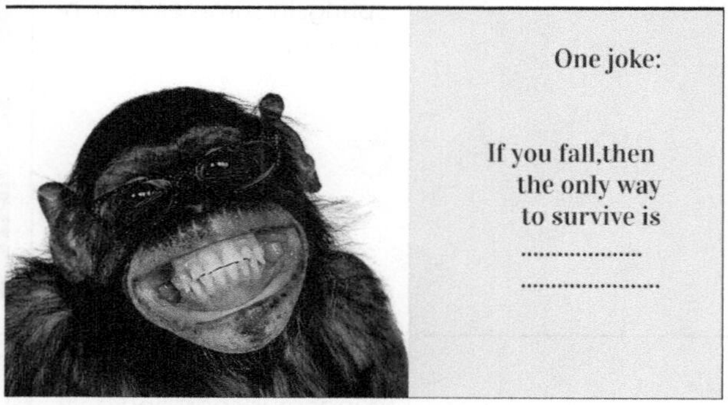
	Thanks for watching! (Fun music playing)	
I loved it! You made a great video, so congratulations. I learned a lot about highlining. And, I can't wait to talk to you about it when I see you in class. I am going to ask you about the webbing and the armsteel rope. All right, great job. Bye-bye!		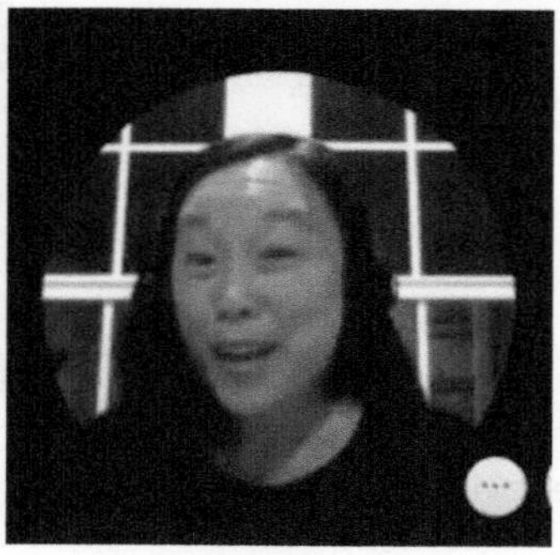

Fig. 6.8 Feedback on student video

This type of feedback takes some time, so you should use it to give individualized feedback when most appropriate. In this case, the teacher is providing a "reaction video," which is a popular genre of social media and gives immediate feedback on each part of the video. If you have a large class of 30 students or more, video feedback could be used to give the whole class feedback on common language errors, or to provide comments on a selection of student projects that are exemplars for students to learn from.

Serve Students a Digital Feedback Cheeseburger

One tool we like to use is the "Feedback Cheeseburger" (Fig. 6.9). It can help you provide specific feedback in a kind way even when your feedback highlights areas that need improvement. Just as a cheeseburger is made up of different components that are arranged in a specific way so that it's appetizing, the Feedback Cheeseburger identifies the different components that feedback should include as well as how to arrange the components so that students are most likely to apply the feedback that they receive.

1. Bun—Relationship Building
2. Cheese—Specific Praise
3. **Meat—Needed Corrections**
4. **Lettuce—General Praise**
5. **Bun—Support**

Fig. 6.9 **The Feedback Cheeseburger**

1. **Relationship Building (Bun):** When providing feedback, it's important to remember that learning is social. This means that you should begin by greeting the student by name and starting with a sentence that helps them feel at ease.

   Example: "Hi Samantha, I hope that everything is going well, and you are enjoying your semester. I just finished reviewing your video job interview and reading your resume. I wanted to provide you with some feedback."

2. **Specific Praise (Cheese):** Once you've greeted the student, you should start your feedback by highlighting what the student has done well. It's important that your praise is specific and grounded in the student's performance.

   Example: "I was impressed at how well you answered the questions and how fluently you were able to speak about your goals and qualifications. Your resume also looked professional and was tailored to this particular job. In both, you used many power verbs from our vocabulary list to highlight your strengths for the job."

3. **Specific Corrections and Recommendations (Meat)**: After providing specific praise, you should highlight specific areas for improvement and provide suggestions for how the student can improve future efforts.

> Example: "I did see a couple of areas that could be improved. First, when you were asked why you were interested in the job, your answer was vague. Although you used power verbs and gave well-prepared answers, it would have been better if you'd highlighted more specific aspects of the job. The interviewer is likely asking the question to see if you are a good fit for the position. In the future, remember that it's always helpful to put yourself in their shoes and try to understand the intent behind the question. Second, at times, it was a little hard to hear your voice. I recommend speaking a little louder and possibly investing in a better microphone."

4. **General Praise (Lettuce)**: After offering critiques and suggestions for improvement, it's important to offer general praise. This reminds the student of the positive aspects of their performance.

> Example: "Aside from that, you did a really nice job in your video interview. I could easily see the hard work that you put into preparing. If this were a real interview, I am sure the interviewer would think you were well prepared and confident. Well done!"

5. **Support (Bun)**: You then want to end with offering support to the student.

> Example: "Please let me know if you have any questions or if additional feedback would be helpful. Have a good weekend!"

Facilitating Quality Peer Feedback

While instructor feedback is important, much of the feedback that students receive is actually from their peers. Peer feedback allows students to receive preliminary feedback before instructor feedback. It also provides an authentic opportunity for students to practice important communication skills. However, peer feedback is frequently unhelpful, or worse, inaccurate. This is especially true with young learners who have not yet developed the skill. Hattie (2008) found that 80 percent of the feedback that primary students received was from peers, but 80 percent of that feedback was inaccurate. One challenge is that peer feedback tends not to provide helpful suggestions for improvement. This is true with students at all levels.

While teachers could ask students to provide their peers with a Feedback Cheeseburger, students tend to do better with simpler models. We recommend two models. "Glow and Grow" is perhaps the simplest model. It tells students to start with specific praise (glow) followed by specific suggestions for improvement (grow).

The second model is the praise-question-polish or "P-Q-P" model (Shin & Crandall, 2014). It is a bit more specific and potentially more helpful to students.

Here are simple instructions that students can use to give each other feedback using the P-Q-P model on any piece of work you have assigned, such as a piece of writing, a project, or a presentation.

1. **P—Praise:** First, tell your classmate at least one thing you liked about their piece. "I liked . . ."
2. **Q—Question:** Then, ask your classmate a question about something you didn't understand in their piece. "Why did you . . ."
3. **P—Polish:** Last, give your classmate one suggestion for "polishing" or making the piece even better. "What about . . ."

When you ask students to provide peer feedback, you should give them a model to follow. For a lower-level writing assignment (Fig. 6.10), you could show students a model of P-Q-P feedback.

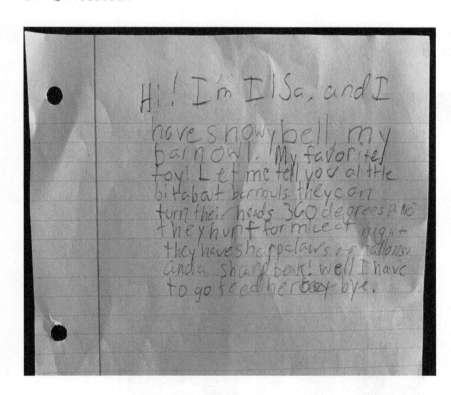

Fig. 6.10
Sample writing assignment by Ilsa

P—Praise: I liked your animal. Barn owls are cool.
Q—Question: Why is her name Snowy Bell?
P—Polish: Do barn owls only eat mice? **Can you add more about** what barn owls eat?

Notice that the teacher has the following sentence starters in blue: *I liked*, *Why*, and *Can you add more about*. These are sentence starters that beginning-level English learners can use to give their peer feedback using P-Q-P. Whether learners are older or younger, at advanced or beginner levels, always provide a model for them to give each other feedback in a positive and productive way.

Examples of Instructor and Peer Feedback

Christine McLaughlin had her fifth-grade students work together to create websites based on a book they chose to read as a group. By creating a website, students were able to collaborate on an authentic project. Christine decided to provide her students with screen-recorded feedback because it would allow her to show the website pages while she described them. She also included a webcam video of herself talking to help create a stronger sense of community with her students and avoid misunderstandings.

Figure 6.11 shows screenshots from a video feedback session along with what was said in the feedback. It's important to note that all of this feedback was provided in a brief, 1 minute and 12 second video. You can see how the visuals supported and provided context for what Christine was saying. Christine was also following the Feedback Cheeseburger in her feedback. She did not suggest a lot of areas for improvement (the Feedback Cheeseburger meat) because the students' work was exemplary. However, the feedback comments highlight how specific feedback can be even when the project meets all or most criteria.

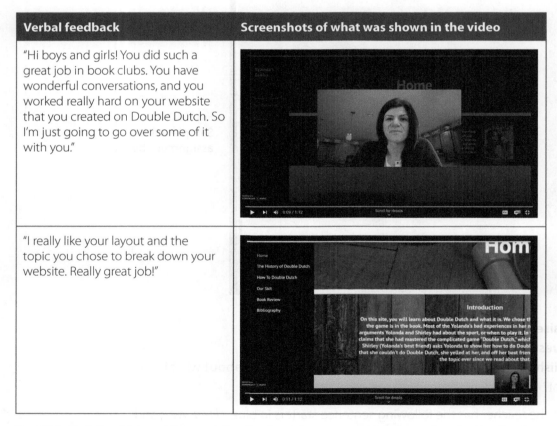

Verbal feedback	Screenshots of what was shown in the video
"Hi boys and girls! You did such a great job in book clubs. You have wonderful conversations, and you worked really hard on your website that you created on Double Dutch. So I'm just going to go over some of it with you."	
"I really like your layout and the topic you chose to break down your website. Really great job!"	

Fig. 6.11 Christine McLaughlin providing feedback in a screen recording, using the Feedback Cheeseburger model (*Continued*)

Verbal feedback	Screenshots of what was shown in the video
"I also like how you include videos and articles. These help us understand the history of Double Dutch. Great job!"	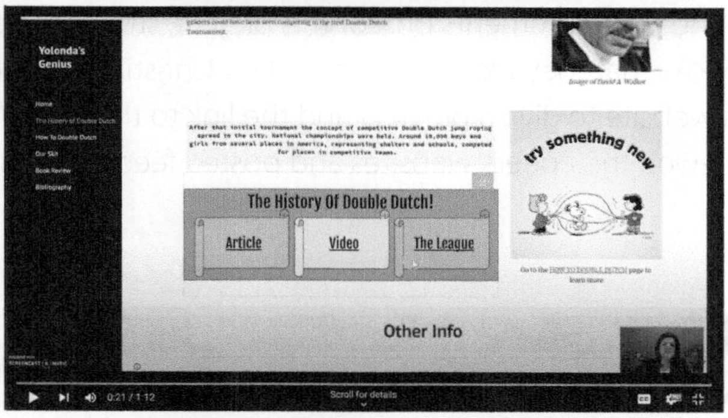
"I also love the images you include. And these other videos here help show us more about Double Dutch. Now I know what I need to do it."	
"This skit that you included going over the book was absolutely phenomenal! Wonderful job! I'm really looking forward to sharing it with our entire class."	
"So one suggestion I have is about the book review. It did not provide details about the book. You could give some examples. That would help us understand your opinion. But overall, fantastic job! I'm here to support you, so if you have any questions, please make sure that you guys come see me. Thank you!"	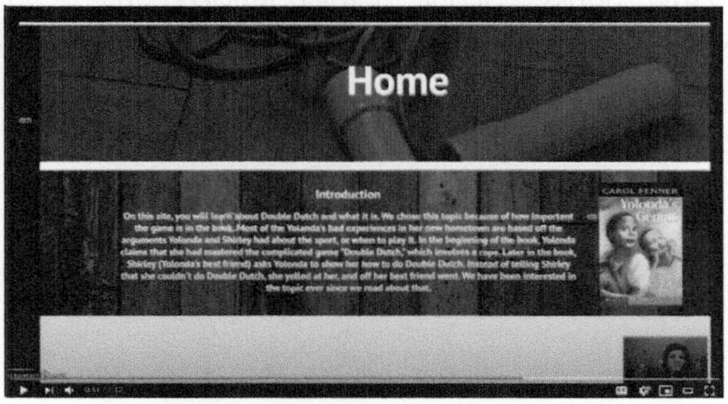

Fig. 6.11 Christine McLaughlin providing feedback in a screen recording, using the Feedback Cheeseburger model

Christine also facilitated peer reviews of the project using the multimedia sharing tool VoiceThread, which allows the creator to upload images, slides, and videos that participants can click through and post comments on. For this project, students created websites on topics based on books that they were reading in class. Christine uploaded screenshots from each group's website to give a preview and the link to the group's website (Fig. 6.12). Students then reviewed their peers' websites and posted feedback comments using audio or video.

Fig. 6.12
Peer review of student-created websites using a multimedia sharing tool

Before allowing students to post their audio or video peer reviews to the VoiceThread, Christine taught them the Glow and Grow method. She emphasized that when providing feedback, they needed to remember to do so in a kind way. This prepared students to provide critical but friendly feedback. One student even replied to the feedback that he received with the following audio comment:

I just wanted to say "Thanks," not only for the positive comments but also for the constructive criticism. That actually really helped and especially people like Keller and Hayden, I think that you guys did a really good job of giving us criticism that wasn't super hard to take. It was really nice to hear so thanks for that because it was really useful.

After You Read

Task 1: Review the challenges you have giving online feedback from the Before You Read section. Then reflect on the following questions based on what you have learned in this chapter.

1. Are the challenges you listed related to making the feedback timely, kind, or specific? What new ideas or tools did you learn about to meet the challenges you listed? Is it more challenging to ensure your feedback is timely, kind, or specific for your teaching context?
2. Could some challenges be addressed by changing the modality of your feedback, that is, by providing text, audio, and/or video feedback? How can changing the modality of your feedback (e.g., from text feedback to video feedback) help your students improve their language learning and increase engagement?

Task 2: In the following table, list different activities or assessments that you typically use to teach English. Then brainstorm various ways to provide students with feedback using different modalities.

Activity or assessment	Text feedback	Audio feedback	Video feedback
Cover letter for a job submitted as a Google doc.	I can ask peers to suggest revisions and add comments to the Google doc. I will provide a rubric that includes expected content, format, and language as a guide.	I could send students screencast recordings showing the Google doc and provide audio feedback while highlighting text and typing comments.	Before the final draft, I could collect the common mistakes from peer feedback and make a short video addressing these mistakes for all students to benefit from.

References

Borup, J., West, R. E., & Thomas, R. A. (2015). The impact of text versus video communication on instructor feedback in blended courses. *Educational Technology Research and Development, 63*(2), 161–184. doi :10.1007/s11423-015-9367-8.

Eraut, M. (2006). Feedback. *Learning in Health and Social Care, 5*(3), 111–118.

Gikandi, J. W., Morrow, D., & Davis, N. E. (2011). Online formative assessment in higher education: A review of the literature. *Computers & Education, 57*(4), 2333–2351.

Hattie, J. (2008). *Visible learning: A synthesis of over 800 meta-analyses relating to achievement.* Routledge.

Shin, J. K., & Crandall, J. A. (2014). *Teaching young learners English: From theory to practice.* National Geographic Learning/Cengage Learning.

Short, D., Becker, H., Cloud, N., Hellman, A., & Levine, L. N. (2018). *The 6 principles for exemplary teaching of English learners: Grades K-12.* TESOL Press.

CHAPTER 7

Be Human

"Nothing is as powerful as the human touch in education."
- GEORGE LUCAS

GOALS

By the end of this chapter, you will be able to:

- explain what it means to "be human" in an online learning environment.
- make a human connection with and among your English learners in an online learning environment.
- explore new ways to be social, present, real, fun, and responsive in the online language learning environment.

A natural interruption during an online meeting

Before You Read

This chapter encourages teachers to "be human" in the online learning environment. What characteristics do you think "being human" as an online English-language teacher involves? Brainstorm some adjectives in this word web that you think describe what it means to be human.

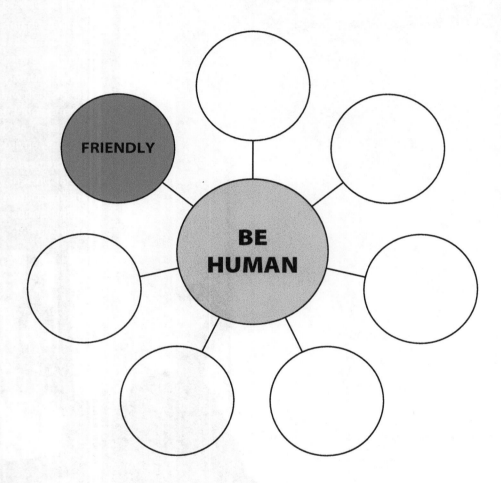

The Importance of Being Human while Teaching

Johnson (2008) explained that there are two aspects of teaching: the academic and the human. Johnson discussed how important the little things are, like being available, listening, instilling a positive outlook, and having fun together. Students' ability to learn and use English would be severely limited if they interacted only with learning materials without frequent opportunities to communicate with, and be supported by, their teacher and peers. After all, language learning is all about communication. Students' potential in language learning is much more likely to be achieved when the human aspects of teaching are strong.

As Richard Culatta, the chief executive officer of the International Society for Technology in Education, says:

> Learning is an inherently social activity, and so often, when we start to move over to online learning, we look at the learning process and we just immediately think of the content. . . . But content [is] just a really thin veneer of the overall education experience, and if . . . the content is the only part that we're making available, it's just not effective learning. (Culatta, 2020)

Culatta goes on to say that teachers should work to develop an online learning environment that is "inclusive of people with a variety of different viewpoints and backgrounds."

Learning English requires meaningful communication with teacher and peers. This can be difficult for many students, but they are more likely to engage meaningfully with others once they feel comfortable and supported. In many ways, it's easier to form a supportive learning environment when students and teachers meet in person for at least part of the time. In fact, when we are with students in person, we form strong communities without thinking much about it. In an online or blended environment, we need to be more intentional in how we strengthen the human aspects of teaching and learning. Online teachers can actually form strong relationships with their students without ever meeting in person. The opposite is also true: when online and blended teachers fail to focus on the human aspects of teaching, their students can be left feeling isolated. Some online students go so far as to say that communicating with their teacher online "feels like you're talking to a robot" (Shin & Borup, 2020). Murphy and Rodriguez-Manzanares (2009) emphasize the need to form a "personal connection so students understand that there is a person behind the computer and not a robot" (p. 8).

The Five BEs of Being Human

We suggest using the "5 BEs" to strengthen the human aspects of online and blended courses: (1) Be Social, (2) Be Present, (3) Be Real, (4) Be Fun, and (5) Be Responsive. In this chapter, we will explore each one and give you a toolbox of ideas to help you "be human" in your teaching.

The 5 BEs

- 🐝 BE SOCIAL
- 🐝 BE PRESENT
- 🐝 BE REAL
- 🐝 BE FUN
- 🐝 BE RESPONSIVE

Be Social

Students can feel nervous and insecure at the start of a course, especially when they are unfamiliar with their teacher or peers. This means that you should work hard at the start of the course to make your students feel comfortable. This is just as true—if not more so—in an online learning environment, where students can feel uncomfortable communicating in new ways using new tools.

ICEBREAKER ACTIVITIES

Social icebreaker activities are a good place to start. Icebreakers are best when they help students to feel comfortable communicating with others online and to learn the communication tools they will be using throughout the course. For instance, if students will be communicating using discussion board forums, then it's helpful to have an icebreaker activity in a discussion board. A common discussion board icebreaker activity is called "Two Truths and a Lie." In the activity, each student posts a text or a video-recorded comment introducing themselves. They say three things about themselves, two that are true and one that's a lie. They then read/watch their peers' comments and reply with a comment guessing which of the three things is a lie and which are true. Once others have posted their guesses, the student posts another comment revealing what their lie actually was and expanding on the two truths. Not only does this type of activity help students to get to know each other, but it also helps students learn how to write comments and reply to others in the discussion board.

Hamed Hashemian in Vietnam does a variation of the "Two Truths and a Lie" activity in his real-time web-conferencing sessions with students, where he introduces himself by listing several "facts" and then asks his students to spot the lie (Fig. 7.1).

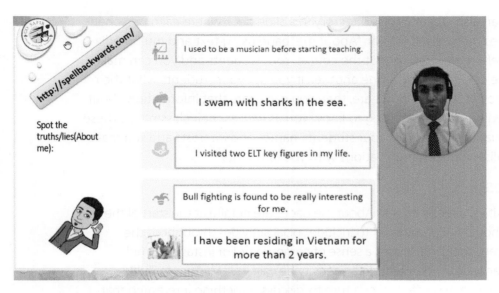

Fig. 7.1 Hamed Hashemian's activity "Two Truths and a Lie"

If you are using a web-conferencing tool, then you should consider which features you are going to use and work them into an icebreaker activity. For instance, if you want students to complete learning activities in breakout rooms, then you can have them do some simple icebreaker activities to practice moving in and out of the rooms. Similarly, you can work other features commonly found in web-conferencing tools, such as polls, interactive whiteboards, and chatboxes, into icebreaker activities. Icebreakers allow students to learn how to use various digital tools in your online environment with low-risk, easy activities that don't require use of new language and content.

ABOUT ME PAGES

If you are using a learning management system (LMS) or another learning platform, it's a good idea to create a "Meet Your Teacher" page. These pages help you introduce yourself to your students, and if you are teaching younger learners, their parents. You could collaborate with colleagues to make a staff directory for learners to look through. Figure 7.2 shows examples from a primary school staff directory that was made once the school moved online due to COVID-19.

Fig. 7.2 Examples of "Meet Your Teacher" pages

Similarly, you can also create a class directory in a slide deck where each person in your class introduces themselves with an "About me" page using text and multimedia that can easily be referred to throughout the course. Your students and you can make a page, so everyone can get to know one another. If you ask your students what their favorite hobbies, movies, and TV shows are, then you can share that information about yourself too. They will appreciate getting to know you as well as their classmates. These pages can be invaluable as you learn your students' names and interests and will make it easier to personalize your communications with your students.

SOCIAL ACTIVITIES

Icebreaker activities, directories, and About me pages are helpful at the start of the semester, but you should also remember to include social activities throughout the semester to help strengthen and sustain a sense of community. For instance, Omid Karden commonly engages his students in an activity he calls "It Is My Turn to Talk" (Fig. 7.3). In the activity, each student takes a turn to "discuss something interesting that happened to them over the past week. If they cannot think of an interesting topic about themselves, they can talk about something interesting they would like to share with their classmates." This is a good example of balancing the human and the academic components of teaching.

Fig. 7.3
Omid Karden's activity "It Is My Turn to Talk"

In Peru, Odalis Monzon Torres creates activities that allow students to share some of their favorite items and toys. Similarly, Ingrid Nicastro in Brazil asks her young students to show and discuss items that are important to them, such as their favorite snack or photos of their family (Fig. 7.4).

Fig. 7.4 Odalis Monzon Torres's learners (left) and Ingrid Nicastro's learners (right) sharing favorite objects

The same principle applies to asynchronous, or on-demand, activities, when instead of sharing in real time, students can record a video for their teacher and peers to watch later. For instance, Erika Cano in Mexico has her students make a video describing their toys using English (Fig. 7.5).

Fig. 7.5 Video by one of Erika Cano's students

While these types of activities are focused on learning and practicing English, the social elements integrated into the activities support and strengthen the human aspects of teaching and learning. This ensures that students do not feel isolated in the online learning environment.

Be Present

Even when you are not physically present with your students, you can still establish a presence by showing yourself in videos and images.

ADDING A PROFILE PICTURE

Learning platforms commonly allow users to add a profile picture. Adding a profile picture only takes a minute and is especially important because that picture will be attached to many of your activities when you post an announcement or comment to a discussion board. In fact, it can be helpful if you change your profile picture periodically—similar to how you may change your profile picture on social media platforms. It can also help you to get to know your students when they upload their own profile picture, so we recommend that you encourage your students to do so at the start of the course.

USING A WEBCAM

When you meet your students with real-time conferencing tools, turn on your webcam so that your students can see you and get to know you better. Before class, take a moment to consider how you are presenting yourself and what's in your background. Strategically placed items such as a family photo or a musical instrument that you play can help you to share something about yourself without ever saying a word. Chapter 8, "Be Aware while You're There," has some helpful tips to remember when you are meeting with students using videoconferencing.

You can also encourage your students to turn on their webcams so that you and others can get to know them more easily. It's important to note, however, that requiring students to leave their webcam on can be problematic. Some students study in areas of their homes that are typically private such as their bedrooms, and they can feel uncomfortable showing those spaces to their teachers and peers. Some video communication tools allow students to use virtual backgrounds that can help them to feel more comfortable since they cover up whatever is in the background. Of course, sometimes students can upload silly or inappropriate backgrounds, which can be a distraction. As with any technology, teachers should set the ground rules for the use of virtual backgrounds and then model for students their appropriate use. For older learners, teachers can co-construct ground rules for the use of virtual backgrounds by selecting a variety of backgrounds that students can use or establishing what types of images are appropriate for class. Of course, if the online environment is brand-new for your learners, you should be ready to lead the discussion of ground rules with your students.

USING VIDEO AND AUDIO IN ASYNCHRONOUS LEARNING

There are many online courses where teachers and students do not communicate in real time. These asynchronous courses tend to rely heavily on text communication. While strong learning communities can be formed using text, it may take longer to do this. Text communications can also be perceived as impersonal and can cause confusion since text lacks important communication cues. With younger students and students with lower proficiency levels still learning to read, it can be challenging to make text-based communication comprehensible. Remember to seek opportunities to communicate using audio or video recordings. For example, in Figure 7.6, Joan Shin prepares students for the next lesson in a quick video that practices the pronunciation of vocabulary words and asks students to bring a leaf to the next class for an activity. The video was recorded on Joan's smartphone using an informal style to make sure students stay connected to her and ready for the next class.

Fig. 7.6
Joan Shin using a video to communicate with students asynchronously

USING VIDEO/AUDIO FOR GIVING FEEDBACK

In Chapter 6, "Focus on Feedback," we discussed how feedback can be provided using video and audio recordings. Not only does this help the teacher to communicate detailed and quality feedback, but it also helps develop a stronger sense of community and connection. Similarly, rather than sending an impersonal email announcement, it may be easier and more effective to send a message in a video recording. This has the added benefit of helping you establish your presence in the course. The goal isn't to replace all or even most text with video recordings, but research has consistently shown that some video recordings can go a long way to forming learning communities (Atwater, Borup, Baker, & West, 2017; Borup, West, & Graham, 2012; Borup, West, & Thomas, 2015; Borup, West, Thomas, & Graham, 2014; Thomas, West, & Borup, 2017).

Be Real

To make a human connection, you can allow students to see how you communicate naturally in English as well as how language is used in the real world. Allowing students to hear you use English naturally, even with some pauses or interruptions, can be OK. It provides a sample of real-life English and may help them feel more comfortable in your class.

BEING NATURAL

Being present in real time or on recorded videos can help you form a more human learning community. However, when speaking in video, teachers and students alike can sometimes feel uncomfortable initially and speak unnaturally as a result. In text, it's easy to write a message and then read it over to correct errors. In video, that's not practical, and if you want to correct something, you need to rerecord the entire message. As a result, it's important to be prepared and have a good idea of what you would like to say before clicking the record button. That said, when you record, everything isn't going to come out of your mouth exactly how you'd like it to. That's normal—embrace it! It's best to only delete a video recording and create a new one when there is something important that needs correcting to prevent student confusion.

MAKING THE MOST OF INTERRUPTIONS

When recording videos or during real-time web-conferencing sessions with your students, there may be unexpected surprises when children suddenly appear in the room or your pet jumps on your lap. These interruptions may feel embarrassing at the time, but research has found that students actually enjoy these types of events because they make their teacher feel more *real*, as students then see their teachers in different ways (Borup, West, Thomas, & Graham, 2014). If you are recording a video to send to your students, you may feel tempted to delete and rerecord after these little unexpected events. Don't try to be perfect in your video recordings. Just be real and be yourself—students will enjoy them more.

TAKING STUDENTS INTO THE REAL WORLD

We can also be real in our videos by taking students out with us into the real world. Smartphones and communication apps have made it easier than ever for teachers to record and send videos anywhere they have a cell signal or Wi-Fi. For instance, when Christine McLaughlin, an elementary school teacher in the United States, was shopping, she took the opportunity to make a video for her students showing and describing the food she was purchasing.

Be Fun

Whenever possible, learning English should be fun. Although your instruction should not prioritize fun over meeting language learning objectives, you can find ways to make your lessons enjoyable for your students. Particularly with remote learning, it can be hard to keep your students focused. Tap into your students' sense of fun. As the teacher, you more than anyone else set the tone, so be creative!

USING FILTERS AND DRESSING UP

When asked what advice she would give to other online and blended teachers, Katherine Haiduchak in Ukraine said, "Be Fun!" One way that she makes her courses more fun is to use video filters. For instance, when teaching students about Halloween, Katherine uses a Halloween filter to get in character (Fig. 7.7).

Fig. 7.7 Katherine Haiduchak using filters at Halloween

If you are not interested in filters, old-fashioned dressing up works well too. For instance, when Kristin Cady notices that her students are experiencing "Zoom-fatigue," she has been known to dress up as Wonder Woman (Fig. 7.8).

Fig. 7.8
Kristin Cady dressing up
to combat students'
Zoom-fatigue

INCLUDING A "FRIEND"

When he began teaching online, Daniel Denisevich knew that he had to make his video lessons fun and engaging for students. He shared this statement: "I had to create a new way to teach kids to interact with each other and learn in a fun environment." One of his solutions was to teach class with his "good friend, Dino." The kids in his class love Dino the Dinosaur and get excited when they interact with their fun friend (Fig. 7.9). Daniel uses a different voice to make Dino come alive and talk directly to his students. He concluded, "By giving Dino to the children, I have created a fun way for kids to learn. With all of us together, the more that kids are interested with Dino and myself, the more they learn." While we don't suggest that all teachers purchase an inflatable dinosaur, it's important that they find their own ways to inject novelty and surprise into their lessons.

Fig. 7.9 Daniel Denisevich's video recording with "Dino the Dinosaur"

USING BITMOJIS

Bitmojis or personal cartoon avatars are popular on social media. You can also use Bitmojis to add some fun to your courses. In fact, some teachers are creating entire Bitmoji classrooms that they place within the LMS or presentations. Bitmoji classrooms commonly have a whiteboard with the agenda and/or learning objectives. Teachers also frequently include a bookshelf with icons that are linked to commonly used tools and resources. Students can access the Bitmoji classroom asynchronously and click on links you set up that lead to your English-language content, like readings, videos, or activities. Figure 7.10 shows Esther Park and her Bitmoji classroom. She added an animated GIF of herself welcoming students to the class and directing their attention to the activities on the whiteboard.

Fig. 7.10 **Esther Park's Bitmoji classroom**

But why stop at creating a classroom when you can create a Bitmoji environment like the coral reef or the rainforest that Virginia Bruno created for her students? (Fig. 7.11) By inviting students into these environments, you can create a fun and creative link to the topic you are teaching.

Fig. 7.11 **Virginia Bruno's Bitmoji environments**

Bitmojis aren't just for young learners. Philippe Petit created a Bitmoji classroom for his university courses (Fig. 7.12).

Bitmoji characters add a little humor and help lighten things up when teaching a new grammar topic for instance. I have noticed that whenever my Bitmoji shows up on screen, it draws my students' interest and they tend to participate more willingly.

Creating a sense of fun by bringing your animated self or by using costumes and filters can help you add a human touch to your instruction. However, don't forget that the concept of fun can be different depending on your culture. Not all of the examples will work in every school, but try to be creative and find ways to bring out your fun side to capture your students' attention.

Fig. 7.12 Philippe Petit's Bitmoji environment for a university course

Be Responsive

Last but not least, you should be responsive. Just as in in-person teaching, when you are teaching in a synchronous session online, it's important to notice how your students are doing and to respond to it. For example, if students seem tired or stressed, you might want to change your plan to change the mood.

RESPONDING TO STUDENT CUES IN LIVE LEARNING SESSIONS

Regardless of the context, teachers need to observe their students and monitor their levels of engagement. In an online learning environment, you might find it more challenging to "read the room," but it's not impossible if you look at your students and notice their facial expressions and behavior. Figure 7.13 is a screenshot from Irmak Yildiz in Turkey who was immediately responsive to her students in class. As she explains:

> I realized that my students were sleepy on a cloudy Monday morning so in order to get their blood flowing first I asked them to do 15 jumping jacks and a few stretching exercises before starting our lesson. They were very happy and surprised and they had a lot of fun because I was also moving with them. I wish that in every country, the students and teachers could start the day with at least 10–15 minute physical exercises. It makes a huge difference! Then, I asked my students to get up and walk around their room to grab an object that they wanted to tell a story about. We practiced both Present Simple and Past Simple tenses without them even realizing it. We are still having online lessons and I can see that my students miss being at school with their friends. To get them to stand up and walk around during a lesson excited them.

Pay close attention to students' behavior and facial expressions during your synchronous sessions. It can also be useful to start every class by finding out how your students are and what their mood is like. (See Chapter 9 for more ideas.)

Fig. 7.13
Irmak Yildiz responding to
students' moods

BEING RESPONSIVE OUTSIDE OF SYNCHRONOUS SESSIONS

Outside of synchronous sessions, you always want to respond when your learners have questions about class. When students reach out with requests for help, it's important that you respond as quickly as possible. When you aren't responsive, students can feel isolated and lose trust in their teacher. As much as you try to be crystal clear with your instructions, students can get lost in the online environment or experience an issue within the LMS. Imagine how frustrating and lonely it can feel if they cannot figure out what to do online! Because you can't be available all day and night, it's best to set clear expectations for how quickly your students should expect a response. After all, teachers need to set boundaries to achieve work–life balance. Letting students know that you are not able to respond to emails after a certain time, but will respond to any issues first thing in the morning, can help lessen their anxiety when they do not hear from you immediately. For example, some teachers let students know that they are not available after 6 p.m. during weekdays or do not answer emails on Sundays. Setting specific boundaries that work for you will help your students have realistic expectations about your availability. Most importantly, be consistent with when and how you follow up. Even when you are teaching students in real time, it can be difficult to respond to all student inquiries in the moment, so remember to follow up with students that you can't help in real time.

Conclusion

There are many ways to add that human touch to your online and blended English-language instruction. We have suggested the "5 BEs" and hope that the examples you have seen will spark some creative ideas for your teaching to (1) Be Social, (2) Be Present, (3) Be Real, (4) Be Fun, and (5) Be Responsive. You might just find that your students will also become social, present, real, fun, and responsive in your class!

After You Read

Think about your current classes and the things you do to create a human connection with your students in online learning environments. For each of the 5 BEs, list some things you already do and come up with new ideas from this chapter that you will start using.

5 BEs	What I already do	What I will start doing
Be Social		
Be Present		
Be Real		
Be Fun		
Be Responsive		

References

Atwater, C. R., Borup, J., Baker, R. E., & West, R. E. (2017). Student perceptions of video communication in an online sport and recreation studies graduate course. *Sport Management Education Journal,* 11(1), 3–12.

Borup, J., West, R. E., & Graham, C. R. (2012). Improving online social presence through asynchronous video. *The Internet and Higher Education,* 15(3), 195–203.

Borup, J., West, R. E., & Thomas, R. A. (2015). The impact of text versus video communication on instructor feedback in blended courses. *Educational Technology Research and Development,* 63(2), 161–184.

Borup, J., West, R. E., Thomas, R. A., & Graham, C. R. (2014). Examining the impact of video feedback on instructor social presence in blended courses. *The International Review of Research in Open and Distance Learning,* 15(3), 232–256.

Culatta, R. (2020). Teaching for better humans 2.0. *TED Radio Hour.* Retrieved from https://www.npr.org/programs/ted-radio-hour/825896890/teaching-for-better-humans-2-0

Johnson, B. (2008). Teacher-student relationships which promote resilience at school: A micro-level analysis of students' views. *British Journal of Guidance & Counselling,* 36(4), 385–398.

Murphy, E., & Rodríguez-Manzanares, M. A. (2009). Teachers' perspectives on motivation in high-school distance education. *Journal of Distance Education,* 23(3), 1–24.

Shin, J. K., & Borup, J. (2020). Making your screen come alive. *InFocus Blog.* National Geographic Learning. Retrieved from https://infocus.eltngl.com/2020/03/24/making-your-screen-come-alive

Thomas, R. A., West, R. E., & Borup, J. (2017). An analysis of instructor social presence in online text and asynchronous video feedback comments. high-school *The Internet and Higher Education,* 33, 61–73.

CHAPTER 8
Be Aware while You're There

"You never really understand a person until you consider things from his point of view."
- HARPER LEE

A man makes sure he's presenting his professional self.

Before You Read

Task 1: Before you begin reading this chapter, think about how you engage your students online in synchronous (real-time) classes, particularly through videoconferencing software (Fig. 8.1). Reflect on the following:

- What do I look like on the screen?

- What are the expressions on my face?

- What gestures do I use?

- What do students see in my background?

- What do I usually have prepared to hold up and show (e.g., objects, books, drawings, and whiteboard)?

- Am I engaging my students on their computer or tablet screen?

Task 2: Are you aware of what your students are experiencing during your online classes? Reflect on the following:

- Can I see or hear all of my students during class?

- How do I know if they are paying attention during class?

- How do I know if they understand or are following my lesson?

- Do I give them opportunities to express themselves before, during, and at the end of class?

Fig. 8.1
Synchronous learning from a student's point of view

The Synchronous Learning Environment

When you teach online, especially if you are teaching synchronously, you should think about what students typically look at on their screens. For a moment, take yourself and your teaching out of the picture. Imagine the types of things your students watch on their TV, computer, tablet, and/or mobile device screens on a daily basis. As you can imagine, they are probably watching all kinds of videos, and probably mostly for entertainment. They may also be playing video games or watching short video clips of people dancing to a popular song or funny memes (animated images or short videos) on social media. Even though you are a teacher and not an entertainer, you have to remember that you are competing with all types of shows and videos. With that in mind, you should always be aware of what you look like and how you are engaging with your students while you are on their screens.

Also, think about what is happening in the home environment. Perhaps family members are working, cooking a meal, or even watching a loud and exciting soccer match on TV. Maybe a dog is barking, a baby is crying, or a car is honking outside an apartment window. There can be any number of distractions competing with your online learning activity when students are in their home environment (Fig. 8.2).

Fig. 8.2
Possible distractions when learning online from home

Knowing that you are competing for students' attention, you will want to set guidelines for your students' home learning environment. You can, of course, ask students to find a comfortable place in front of a computer without distractions. With young learners, you can also ask parents to set up a space where their children can focus on their screen and get up and move around for activities like games or songs. Unfortunately, you cannot assume that your students will be able to find a location free from distractions in their homes. Even if you have guidelines for students (and parents) for the home learning environment, you will have far less control of the environment than in a traditional class.

However, you can control the quality of your instruction and how you manage the synchronous learning environment.

How to Use Your Webcam Effectively

A good place to start when setting up your synchronous learning environment is with your webcam. When you are preparing to teach online or even recording a video for your students to watch later, always "be aware while you're there." In other words, consider some practical aspects of how you present yourself. For example, pay attention to the lighting, the angle of your camera, your eye contact, your facial expressions and gestures, and your distance from the camera. Here are some simple tips for setting up and using your webcam effectively:

1. Set up a soft or indirect light in front of you. Make sure the light is not directly behind you or pointing directly at your face. Sitting in front of a window in the daytime can create different effects in front of or behind you, so it's important to be mindful of light sources both inside and outside your room. If your students cannot see you clearly, it can be distracting for them.

2. Position the webcam at eye level. This is usually the most flattering and comfortable placement. The webcam shouldn't be too high or too low. Sometimes, simply putting your laptop or tablet on a pile of books is all you need to get your webcam to eye level.

3. Look into the webcam as much as possible. Now that your webcam is at eye level, make eye contact with your students through the webcam. This can be challenging because you might be looking at your students or your presentation slides on the screen. You may be checking the chatbox located at the bottom of your computer screen or checking your lesson plan on your desk. Try to make sure you look into your webcam as much as possible. This will help your students feel more connected to you.

4. Use facial expressions and gestures to engage your students. In addition to making eye contact, it's important to enhance your instruction with pleasant and natural facial expressions and gestures. As English-language teachers, we often use facial expressions and gestures to help make language input comprehensible. However, in an online learning environment, we have to draw students into our class through the webcam. Be aware of your facial expressions and movement to create the most comfortable, inviting, and engaging class. If smiling is a common and culturally appropriate way to make students feel comfortable in your class, then make sure you are smiling right into the camera! If hand and arm gestures are a common form of nonverbal communication, then be sure your webcam is positioned in a way to show them off well.

5. Sit at a comfortable distance from the webcam that shows your head and shoulders. Imagine you are talking to someone in person, for example, sitting across from someone at a table in a café. In person, we never sit so close to people that we can only see someone's face. At the distance across a café table, we usually see people's faces and shoulders. Many people use hand and arm gestures while

talking. Imagine your students looking at you through the webcam. They will feel more comfortable seeing you as if you are at this distance (see Fig. 8.3).

Fig. 8.3
Head and shoulders on a webcam

Next we will look at some common webcam mistakes that you should avoid so that students can see you clearly on their screen (Table 8.1).

Common Webcam Mistakes

The Silhouette If you sit with your back to a window or another main source of light, the light can create a silhouette and make your face hard to see.	
The Zebra If you sit facing a window with blinds, you may end up with stripes on your face.	
The Haunting If you are teaching at night, have enough light in the room or you might end up looking scary.	
The Close Talker If you sit too close to the webcam, you can make your students feel very uncomfortable.	

Table 8.1 Common webcam mistakes (*Continued*)

The Social Distancer If you sit too far away from the webcam, your students may have a hard time seeing your expressions and making a connection with you. An exception might be when you use physical gestures and need to show your whole body.	
The "Nosey" Professor If you put your device on your lap, your students may end up having a good view up your nose, and your device may move around too much during the session.	
The Toddler If your device is too high, students might not see parts of your face that are important for making a connection.	
The Profiler If you use two computers or monitors, make sure that you are almost always facing your students in a synchronous session or students may not feel a connection with you.	
The Reader If you read from your notes frequently and don't make eye contact, students may not feel a connection with you.	

Table 8.1 Common webcam mistakes

How to Enhance the Space behind and around You

Another way to manage the online learning environment is making the space around you reflect your personality and be conducive to learning. Your students will not only see you through the webcam but also see what's in the background. There are many ways to prepare your background to enhance students' learning while also allowing your personality to shine through the screen.

Let's first consider reflecting your personality. Something as simple as photographs or objects that are meaningful to you can help your students get to know you better. Depending on your culture or even requirements from your school or institution, you may or may not want to reveal certain details about yourself and your home life. Therefore, you should carefully curate the space behind and around you to reflect who you are. if you know your audience is adult learners interested in English literature, you might place yourself in front of your bookcase (Fig. 8.4).

Fig. 8.4 Curating your webcam background

Depending on the videoconferencing platform you use, you might be able to enhance your image on the screen. Some platforms have virtual backgrounds, so it looks as if you are in space or sitting in a nice, clean room with appropriate decor behind you. Some have fun filters that allow you to have glasses, a hat, or animal features. These could be useful when you want to play a character from a book. You can put on a filter of a pirate with a hat and eye patch when reading about Blackbeard. Maybe you want to demonstrate a dialogue between a man and woman. If you are female, you could read the lines by the female character with no filter and then put a mustache filter on when reading the part of the male character. In the latter example, not only would this make the role-play demonstration more engaging, but also the filter would help students follow the dialogue and improve their comprehension.

Virtual backgrounds also allow you to upload images to enhance your teaching. You may want to put the page of your textbook behind you or an image you want to discuss. For example, in Figure 8.5 the teacher is able to talk about the unit opener page for "Awesome Animals" and use the background as an integral part of her instruction. She is pointing to the unit objectives in the box to get students ready for the new unit. In addition, she can move to the side and give students some time to look at the photo and generate an interesting discussion. Virtual backgrounds can also be used to inspire students' creativity and imagination. If you are learning about how to order food in different types of restaurants, you can prepare backgrounds representing a fancy restaurant, a fast-food restaurant, or a casual pizza place.

Fig. 8.5
Using a unit opener page as a virtual background

Once you have set up your webcam and background, you are ready to think about effective ways to present material in the online learning environment.

How to Present New Language

As you develop your lessons, you should brainstorm all the different ways you can teach the lesson content, for example, the vocabulary and grammar. Then analyze which one will be the best choice for your online learning environment. For example, if you are teaching a unit on food, you can present the vocabulary in a variety of ways (Table 8.2).

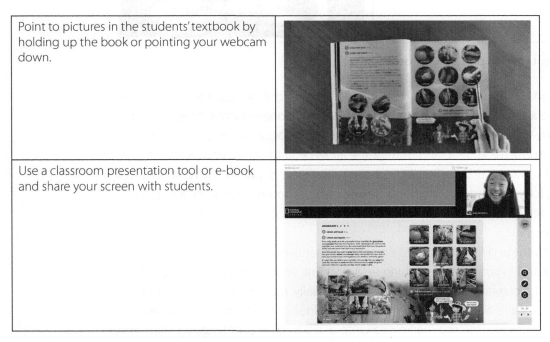

| Point to pictures in the students' textbook by holding up the book or pointing your webcam down. | |
| Use a classroom presentation tool or e-book and share your screen with students. | |

Table 8.2 **Different ways to present the vocabulary of food** (*Continued*)

Hold up picture cards of each food item.	
Take pictures of food or find images on the Internet and create a slide presentation. Then share your screen with students.	
Show realia or real food from your kitchen or garden.	

Table 8.2 **Different ways to present the vocabulary of food**

Each way can be used to effectively teach your students the names of food in English. You can also use a combination of them. If you are teaching online from home, why not use real food? We usually use picture cards in the classroom because we cannot always carry or show the real thing. Teaching from home allows you to set up your webcam in the kitchen and show the real food item from the refrigerator or pantry. This can be much more engaging for your students. If you can see students through a webcam too, they can also go to their kitchen and find food that matches the vocabulary in the unit to show their comprehension.

In addition to these different ways to present new language, you will want to have a whiteboard on hand in your online learning environment. Whiteboards are an important teaching tool in the classroom, both in person and virtually. Many videoconferencing software platforms have electronic whiteboards embedded. If this feature is available to you, you can use different-colored markers to write or draw to present language and make input comprehensible. It can also be convenient to have an actual whiteboard nearby to grab and show students how to write a letter or word and even draw a picture to make a word or idea comprehensible. Table 8.3 shows these two uses of a whiteboard.

Write or draw on a small whiteboard and hold it up to the webcam.	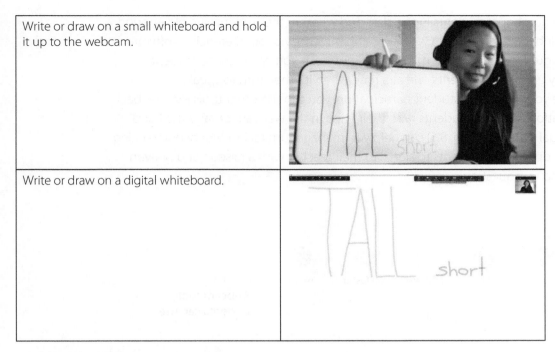
Write or draw on a digital whiteboard.	

Table 8.3 **Two uses of a whiteboard**

Whiteboards can be used by both teachers and students to communicate quickly and easily through the webcam. Students can use whiteboards to write down their answers or ideas to share with the teacher and other classmates. If possible, ask your students to have a whiteboard handy for online classes. For teachers of young learners, it can be very helpful to use physical whiteboards or even hold up pen and paper since young children are still learning to write English letters and need to build those fine motor skills. With older learners who can type quickly and easily, digital whiteboards and chatboxes may be all you need.

Once you make decisions about where you will teach, where you will set up your computer or tablet, how you will position your webcam, and what kinds of materials you will need to create an engaging synchronous class, be sure you set everything up before your class starts. This is no different from going in person to your brick-and-mortar classroom and preparing your classroom environment before your students arrive. It might be only 10–15 minutes before the start of class, but this can help ensure that your virtual classroom, including your webcam and background, is all set up and ready for the lesson.

How to Get Feedback from Students

For learning to be successful, communication between teacher and students must be two-way. Just as in an in-person class, you should consider how you will hear from your students in an online environment. Fortunately, current technology allows for this two-way communication. When students have their webcams on, they can participate in some traditional ways. If you can see all students in their webcams at the same time, you can call on students who raise their hand just as in an in-person class. However, you need to consider the number of students in the class and whether the students are old enough to manage their behavior with both webcams and mics on. Videoconferencing software usually allows you to control whose mic is on or muted, so you can manage student participation by unmuting students one at a time when it's their turn to speak.

To increase your control of student participation, you can use other tools like feedback icons in the platform. Having students raise their hand in the webcam or raise the hand icon in the virtual classroom (Fig. 8.6) can help you manage turn taking. Videoconferencing platforms have options for students to signal to their teacher with a raised hand or even answer yes or no to a question.

Fig. 8.6
Webcam tools students can use

You might also encourage your students to use hand gestures with simple sign language to make synchronous sessions more interactive. Figure 8.7 shows some frequently used hand gestures in the United States that help teachers see right away if students have a question, agree with what was said, or have an answer. This is more specific than raising a hand and can help you unmute students more judiciously.

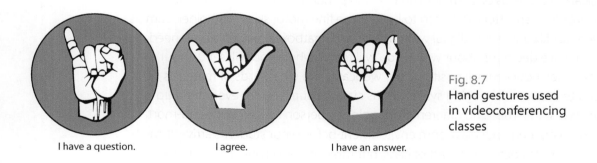

I have a question.   I agree.   I have an answer.

Fig. 8.7
Hand gestures used in videoconferencing classes

Naturally, appropriate hand signals vary from culture to culture, so you should feel free to select hand gestures that make sense in your country or culture. Just be consistent!

You can also use the sign language alphabet to go over answers to multiple-choice or matching questions. Even if all students are muted, you can still check their comprehension. In fact, this technique could work when you are teaching in person as well since it can help you check comprehension of all learners, not just the few who like to speak out frequently. It's very simple for students to learn the first four letters of the sign language alphabet. Figure 8.8 shows the letters A, B, C, and D in American Sign Language.

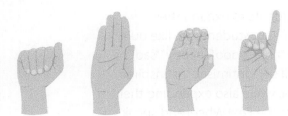

Once students are used to these four letters, they can show their answers to any multiple-choice activity. You can say, "OK, students. What is the answer to number one?" Then look at each student and see if they are holding up their hand to the camera showing A, B, C, or D in sign language.

Of course, the chatbox is another option for getting feedback and answers from students, and this can be used often to encourage participation and interaction. However, sometimes this strategy can take more time or be more difficult to use. If all students type into the chatbox at once, the answers can fly by so quickly that you may not be able to keep track of who answered and who did not, never mind who answered correctly. Try it and see what works best for the different parts of your synchronous class time.

How to Do Routine Checks to Create a Positive Learning Environment

Finally, when you are teaching online and trying to manage the synchronous learning environment, it's a good idea to check in frequently with students. This will help you know which students may be losing focus, having difficulties with the lesson, or needing more support or attention.

Log in Early

If possible, log in early to class and set up your webcam and all the materials you need to make your class successful, as suggested in the previous section. Logging in early can also give you some valuable time with a few students. If you make it a routine and let students know, you can make meaningful connections with your students before class starts. It's important to establish a good relationship with students in a virtual environment so that they know you are there with them. Some students will log in early anyway, and you can check in on how they feel, answer any questions they may have, or ask them any questions you may have. It's a great way to be aware of your students' individual needs. You can enhance the atmosphere by playing some fun, upbeat, or relaxing music before the class begins. You might even ask students at the beginning of your course what music or songs they like and make a playlist for their class.

Greet Students

Before you start the lesson, take a moment to greet students and see how they are. This helps you be aware while you are there! Knowing how students are feeling and allowing them an opportunity to express themselves can get your online class off to a great start.

The Feel Wheel (Fig. 8.9) is a great way to encourage students to expand their vocabulary in English when they talk about how they feel. If your students are like ours, they use the same few adjectives to describe how they are: "fine," "good," "happy," "sad," or "tired." Instead of saying, "I feel happy today," maybe they will say "optimistic" or "inspired," which will give you an even better idea about how they feel, while also expanding their vocabulary. You can ask students to choose descriptors from the Feel Wheel and speak, type into the chatbox, or even write the word down on a piece of paper and hold it up (Fig. 8.10). Based on your students' level, you can simplify the wheel to include only the two inner circles or even change the words on the outer circle. Just be sure you include words that your students have learned previously and add new words as you learn them.

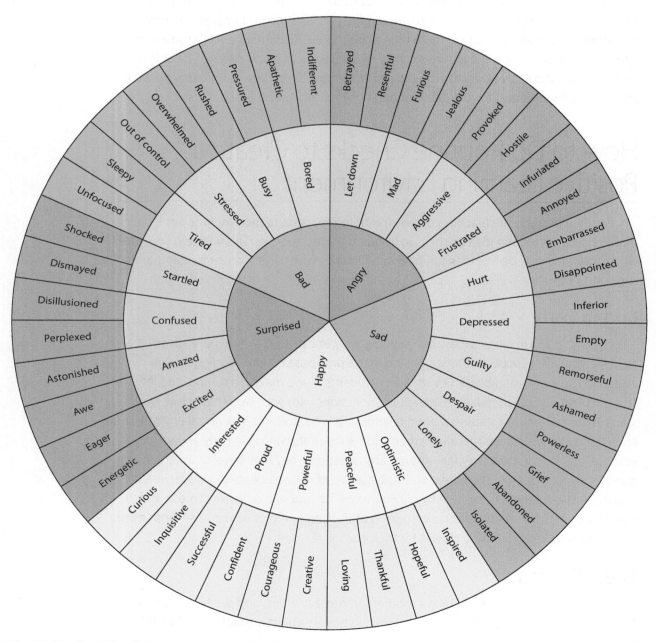

Fig. 8.9 The Feel Wheel

Fig. 8.10
A class using the Feel Wheel

Pulse Checks and Exit Checks

A pulse check is a strategy for teachers to quickly see how students are feeling during class. Basically, you are checking in with them by asking a question or a few questions. You might want to take a pulse check based on a specific activity at any time during class. An exit check means you check in with students at the end of class. It will help you be aware of how your students are doing. Teachers can use sign language to take a quick pulse check. Just be specific about what each sign language letter means. See Figure 8.11 for an example of how to find out if students liked a story or not.

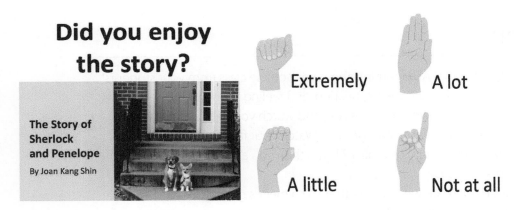

Fig. 8.11 Using gestures for a pulse check

Some teachers like to use hand waving to see how students feel about an activity: "Wave one hand if you liked this activity. Wave two hands if you *really* liked this activity. Don't wave if you didn't like it!" Depending on how many students you have, their ages, and their preferences, you can find the appropriate nonverbal signals to get useful feedback. These nonverbal communications can also increase students' attention and interaction.

You could also take a poll, which is a common feature in videoconferencing platforms. A poll is a good pulse check when you have a large number of students in your class (e.g., lecture). Figure 8.12 shows the results of a poll for a large class. Here the instructor wanted to see how good or bad students' Internet connections were.

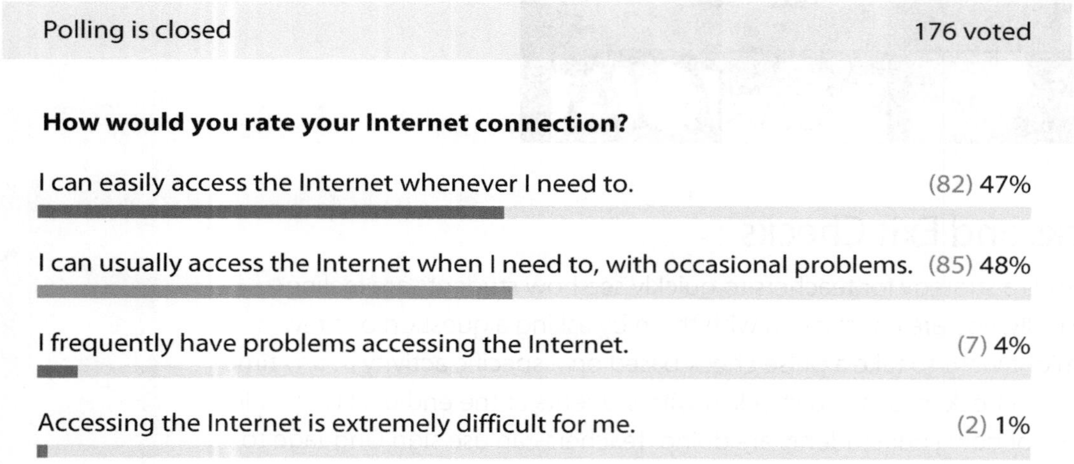

Polling is closed	176 voted

How would you rate your Internet connection?

I can easily access the Internet whenever I need to. (82) 47%

I can usually access the Internet when I need to, with occasional problems. (85) 48%

I frequently have problems accessing the Internet. (7) 4%

Accessing the Internet is extremely difficult for me. (2) 1%

Fig. 8.12 **Results of a poll done with a university class**

Conclusion

Be aware while you're there! Always think about your online class from your students' point of view: imagine what they are seeing, hearing, and feeling as they watch you on their screen. Try recording your own online session, and watch yourself as if you are one of your students. Look at what is in the background. Watch your facial expressions and gestures. Did you make your screen come alive? If yes, then you are one step closer to engaging your learners in English!

Don't forget that being aware while you're there also means getting feedback from your students. Find ways to check in with them during your synchronous sessions. It's important to find ways to get feedback throughout the class, whether by using technology or with creative nonverbal strategies. You can check individual students' understanding of language input as well as check the pulse of your whole class. This kind of feedback will help you make your lessons come alive!

After You Read

Task 1: Record a synchronous class session (with permission from your students and/or parents). Use the recording to observe yourself teaching. Based on what you learned in this chapter, determine if you were successful in being aware while you were there!

Were you aware while you were there?
Did you use your webcam effectively to engage learners during the synchronous session?
Did you present language effectively using the webcam and other features of your videoconferencing platform?
Did you use a variety of strategies to get immediate feedback from students?
Did you do any pulse checks with students to enhance your instruction?

Task 2: Take a look at an upcoming lesson that will be done completely or partially in a synchronous online session through videoconferencing. What language and skills are you teaching in that lesson? What types of activities are you planning to do?

Lesson topic: _____ **Target language (vocabulary, grammar, language skill):** _____ **Lesson objectives:** _____	
What are one or two ways you can engage your learners visually in this particular lesson through your videoconferencing platform?	
What are one or two ways you can present the new language in your lesson using the webcam and other features of your videoconferencing platform?	
What are one or two strategies you can use to get immediate feedback from students on this lesson through your videoconferencing platform?	
What are one or two ways you can do pulse checks with students to enhance your instruction?	

CHAPTER 9

Lighting the Fire of Motivation for Students Online

"Education is not filling a bucket, but lighting a fire."
- WILLIAM BUTLER YEATS

Friends gather around a campfire.

Before You Read

Before you begin reading this chapter, think about one of the most motivating lessons you have taught online or facilitated using online applications in a blended classroom. Fill out this graphic organizer to help you reflect on your experience with this lesson.

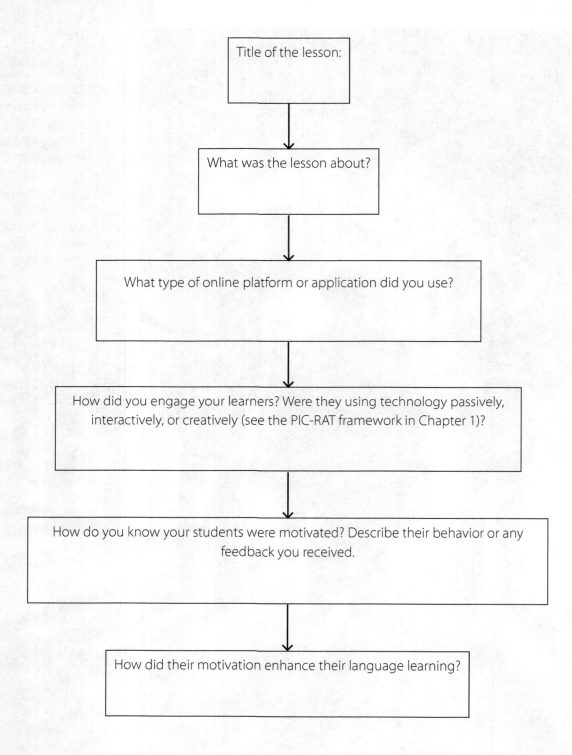

Title of the lesson:

What was the lesson about?

What type of online platform or application did you use?

How did you engage your learners? Were they using technology passively, interactively, or creatively (see the PIC-RAT framework in Chapter 1)?

How do you know your students were motivated? Describe their behavior or any feedback you received.

How did their motivation enhance their language learning?

Introduction

It's important that teachers work to motivate students in any environment, but it becomes even more important in online or blended courses where students tend to have more opportunity to slip through the cracks. Research has repeatedly shown that students are less likely to pass their online courses than their in-person courses (Bawa, 2016; Freidhoff, 2020). The reasons behind the lower pass rates in online courses are complex, but many students lack the self-regulation and self-motivational skills needed to thrive in a more flexible learning environment.

The common saying "You can lead a horse to water, but you can't make it drink" describes what we can't control when it comes to student motivation. Perhaps a better analogy was given by the late Sir Ken Robinson:

> Every farmer and gardener knows that you cannot make a plant grow. You cannot do that. You don't stick the roots on and paint the petals and attach the leaves. The plant grows itself. What you do is provide the conditions for growth, and great farmers know what the conditions are and bad ones don't.

Like gardeners, teachers of blended and online courses need to set the conditions for their students to grow and learn. This can be challenging for teachers who are new to this environment because they have to learn to motivate students at a distance. This requires different strategies than motivating students in person. In this section, we will share how motivation theory can be practically applied to online and blended courses.

Sources of Motivation

A student's motivation is largely determined by two variables (see Wigfield & Eccles, 2000):

- **Value** (i.e., usefulness, importance, and interest) that a student places on mastering the subject material and skills.

- **Expectations** that a student has for being successful in a learning activity.

Thankfully, the value that students place on learning and expectations of success can change and be influenced by teachers. Bandura (1977), the renowned psychologist and researcher, found that a student's expectations for success (what he called self-efficacy) are influenced primarily by the following four factors:

1. **Emotions:** Students are more confident in their ability to succeed when they are experiencing positive emotions (i.e., excitement, curiosity, and comfort) compared to negative emotions (i.e., stress, confusion, and anxiety).
2. **Models:** Students have more belief in their ability to be successful when they have seen peers succeed at the task. This allows students to say, "If they can do it, I can do it."
3. **Encouragement:** Students' confidence grows when others whom they respect and know offer encouragement. The encouragement has the most impact when it is grounded in students' actual abilities.
4. **Mastery:** If students have mastered similar tasks previously, they will be much more confident in their ability to succeed. Of the four sources, students' previous experiences mastering tasks have the greatest impact on their expectancy of future success.

The same motivational principles can be seen in nearly all aspects of life, including learning to speak English. Your students likely see the value of speaking English. Even if they don't enjoy the act of learning and practicing English, they—especially older students—can probably see the social and economic benefits of learning the language—and in the case of young learners, economic benefits may be in the form of stickers or prizes from the teacher. Language learning motivation is often described as either instrumental or integrative (Gardner, 1985). If your students have instrumental motivation, they want to learn English for practical reasons such as getting good grades, pleasing their parents, getting a job, or getting into a good university. With this type of motivation, you can set the right conditions by incorporating materials aligned with your students' reasons for learning English.

If your students have integrative motivation, they want to learn English to understand and get to know people who speak it. With English's status as a global language, many students may be motivated if learning language is connected to authentic communication with other speakers of English around the world. Such communication may be for traveling to different countries around the world and using English as a lingua franca, for interacting with people around the world through video games, or for communicating with people globally through social media. Students' motivation is unlikely to be purely instrumental or purely integrative; instead, one is likely to be more dominant than the other in any individual. The key is identifying what types of motivation you can tap into with students in your English class. It can be related to the type of class you teach, the age of your learners, or even individual learners' interests and needs.

At the same time, learning a language can be challenging, and students can lack confidence in their ability to master English. Dörnyei (2014) describes students' "L2 motivational self-system," which consists of three aspects:

1. *Ideal L2 self*: the English-speaking person a student would like to become, such as an English-speaking businessperson traveling internationally.
2. *Ought-to self:* the attributes an English student believes they ought to have because of personal or social obligations, such as pressure from parents to be a good student.
3. *L2 learning experience:* the motivation of an English student specific to the immediate learning environment and experience, such as how enjoyable a class is or how successful they feel in the class.

We can set conditions for motivating students, particularly by enhancing their L2 learning experience, as described by Dörnyei (2014). Students who are new to online or blended learning can lack confidence in their ability to thrive in these types of environments. This may affect their ought-to self if they are not sure what to do to be successful. It might also create some confusion if they cannot connect to their ideal L2 self through the course. Fortunately, we can help students to build confidence in their ability to learn English and to connect to their motivational self-system in online and blended environments. The next section outlines some useful strategies.

Strategies for Increasing Student Motivation

In order to keep your English language students motivated in online and blended learning environments, you can apply some simple strategies that will create the conditions for your students to grow and learn.

Focus First on Relationships

The importance of fostering caring relationships with and between students cannot be overstated. Relationships can create a positive L2 learning experience, enhancing the motivation that students already have and sparking a new interest in learning English. Positive relationships will naturally increase the value that students place on learning English and their desire to be successful in your course. These relationships will also have a calming effect on students who are anxious about learning English in an online or blended environment, as encouragement is more impactful once students know and trust the person providing it. Similarly, peers that students know and trust and who model success can increase students' confidence that they too can be successful. Even when the learning is challenging, a sense of community between students can give them a "we-are-in-this-together" feeling that helps them to persevere through difficult activities.

Monika Bandi from Romania shows how she built the confidence of her young learners with a language activity that allowed them to share something personal about themselves. Monika knows her learners are eager to share their favorite toy, but she also wants to practice grammar in her lesson. As Monika explains, "We decided to review prepositions of place by using one of our small favorite toys and two cups or two plastic glasses from their household. At first, I demonstrate the task, that is, by telling the students a sentence using a preposition of place and at the same time showing it to them with the cups and the toy. I repeated this several times, and then the students were asked to do the same thing" (Fig. 9.1).

Fig. 9.1 Monika Bandi's activity combining sharing something personal with a grammar focus

Even with older learners, sharing something personal in a lesson can create a sense of comfort and community, and integrating students' sharing into a language practice activity makes repetition and practice of a language form more meaningful. For more ideas on how to focus on relationships, see Chapter 7, "Be Human."

Leverage Students' Interests

As with any subject, some students have a natural interest in learning English and some don't. Even when students don't naturally enjoy learning English, they may become more interested in learning English when the teacher integrates their personal and/or professional interests into learning activities. For example, in a class of adults who are learning English for business, incorporating communication skills for running a successful meeting, making a formal proposal presentation, or conducting a marketing survey could be highly motivating. These activities can tap into your students' instrumental motivation to work effectively in a company. Or, if you are teaching a class of university students who have an integrative motivation to communicate with people around the world, you could tap into their motivation by finding some interesting bloggers or vloggers who produce content in English that you think your students will enjoy, for them to respond to. For example, if your students are interested in a particular movie, you could find a couple of vloggers who do movie reviews in English and have your students compare them, post comments, and even create their own review.

Ingrid Nicastro from Brazil knows how to enhance her students' learning experience by tapping into their interests. Her students love superhero movies, so she grabbed their attention by showing them a short movie clip from a Spider-Man movie. She then tested their language skills by asking questions about the clip. Simple adjustments such as these can have a big impact on students' motivation (Fig. 9.2).

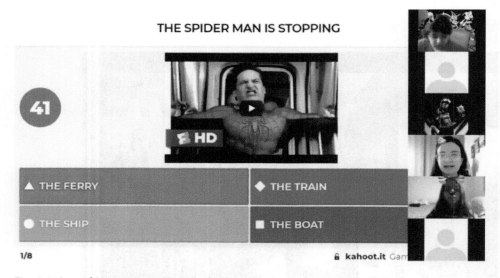

Fig. 9.2 Ingrid Nicastro motivating learners with a quiz using a clip from a Spider-Man movie

If you are in a fully online environment, it can be more difficult to recognize and learn your students' interests. Icebreaker activities can help you get to know your students and their interests (see Chapter 7, "Be Human"), but a simple survey can also help you more directly learn your students' interests and the kinds of activities they enjoy. There are many free online survey software programs you can use. Figure 9.3

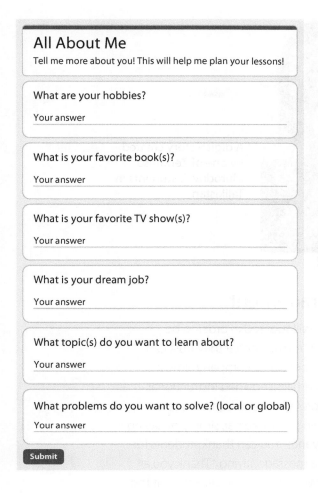

All About Me
Tell me more about you! This will help me plan your lessons!

What are your hobbies?

Your answer

What is your favorite book(s)?

Your answer

What is your favorite TV show(s)?

Your answer

What is your dream job?

Your answer

What topic(s) do you want to learn about?

Your answer

What problems do you want to solve? (local or global)

Your answer

Submit

Fig. 9.3
Sample survey questions

shows some sample questions you might want to ask your students to find out what they are interested in. The design of your survey will depend on the age and language level of your students. For young children, you might give the survey via their parents.

Throughout the course, you can also get to know your students as they practice English. For instance, Zeboniso Murodova in Tajikistan worked with teenage students in an after-school program to create digital stories about their lives. Her students' personal stories were very emotional and even showed many hardships. However, they also told stories of strength and hope. Zeboniso wrote, "These first five girls whom I involved became so motivated and they conducted a cascading workshop for 12 of their peers at school. My own and the participants' digital stories were exported and downloaded to flash drives and the participants have the intention of sharing the product of their work with family and peers individually." By creating digital stories, not only did her students learn storytelling and digital literacy skills, but also Zeboniso learned about her students in more depth and found even more ways to inspire and motivate them (Fig. 9.4).

Fig. 9.4
A digital story created by one of Zeboniso Murodova's students in Tajikistan

Provide and Facilitate Regular Encouragement

As explained earlier, students need to believe that they will succeed in order to be motivated. When students lack confidence, encouragement from a teacher they trust can help them to believe in their ability to succeed. Encouragement can accompany almost any interaction with students (e.g., course announcements, emails, recorded instructional videos, and live video class sessions). For instance, you can provide encouragement to an entire group of students by welcoming them at the beginning of a webinar, simply by saying, "Thank you for attending today's class. It's great to see everyone!" You can thank students for their collective performance, for example, with an email or a message saying, "Thank you all for submitting your vocabulary review last week. We had 100 percent of the class submit the assignment!" If you wish to improve participation levels, you can start a webinar by praising students' attendance, and if you wish to increase assignment submissions, you could send out a class announcement thanking students for submitting their work. Encouragement is most impactful when it is individualized and customized to the student. You might start a webinar early so that you can welcome individual students by name the moment they log in: "Welcome to class, Fatima. It's great to see you again!" And at certain times during the semester, you can acknowledge individual students' sustained efforts in direct emails, for example, "Fatima, thank you for submitting your vocabulary review. That makes an entire month without any missing work!"

It can help to think about when students are most likely to feel unsure about their ability to succeed. At the start of the semester, students can feel apprehensive, so it's helpful to welcome students to the course to encourage them to engage in learning activities and contact you when they need help. It is especially important to provide encouraging feedback to students on their first few assignments—but this does not mean you should give empty praise. Your feedback should be grounded in students' work. If you need to provide corrective feedback, wrap it in praise and encouragement. This is important even with adults. Researchers Losada and Heaphy (2004) examined the performance of teams in a business and found that the biggest indicator of a successful team was the ratio of positive to negative comments. Specifically, they found that in highly successful teams, there were 5.6 positive comments for every negative one. For average-performing teams, the ratio was 1.9 positive comments for every negative one, and in the low-performing team, the ratio was flipped, with nearly 3 negative comments for every positive comment. While we can't necessarily generalize this research to language learning, what is clear is that comments of praise and encouragement should outnumber negative comments.

Even when students are engaging in their course and submitting work, they can still feel discouraged and need more encouragement. It's relatively easy to see student frustration or discouragement in an in-person environment. In asynchronous courses that rely on text communication, it can be more difficult to recognize student frustration because you lack cues that convey emotion. To overcome this limitation, it can be helpful to occasionally have students communicate using video recordings or live video class sessions. Another strategy is to regularly do pulse checks and exit checks (see Chapter 8) using short surveys that students complete before they sign off from a synchronous class session or when they submit an assignment. Longer mid-course evaluations or reflections can also help to identify those students who need extra encouragement. You can ask students to record video comments so that you can see frustration or satisfaction on your students' faces and hear it in their voices more easily.

Lastly, as students finish your course, consider having them record a video for future students, providing them with recommendations and encouragement. For instance, when students graduate from our Master's program, we ask them to post videos to an online video discussion tool, Flipgrid, which are shared with incoming students the next semester (Fig. 9.5).

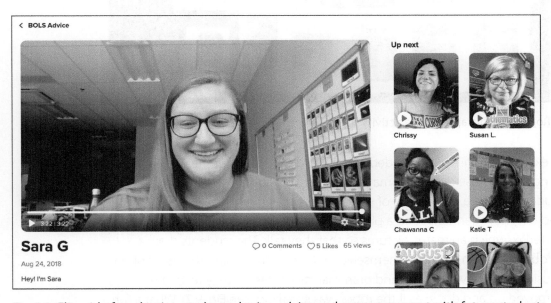

Fig. 9.5 Flipgrid of graduating students sharing advice and encouragement with future students

Add Novelty and Variety

Students are naturally drawn to new experiences, and new technology can have what's called a "novelty effect": students are typically more engaged in an online learning activity the first time they experience the technology. Having said this, we need to remember to use technology not solely for the purpose of using technology, but to pair technology with meaningful learning activities. And so, while the novelty effect tends to be temporary, the interest can be sustained if the activity is meaningful in itself.

You can also add novelty in the way that you present the learning activities. For instance, Scarlet Rojas in Peru knew that her students would be more motivated to engage in a learning activity if she focused it on a "zombie apocalypse and how to survive." While the novelty of a zombie apocalypse motivated students to engage in the activity, the focus of the activity was still on using vocabulary and expressing opinions in English (Fig. 9.6).

Fig. 9.6 Scarlet Rojas's zombie apocalypse activity

In another example, Monika Bandi added novelty and excitement to her class by having her young learners use recyclable materials to create robots. After they created their robots, students wrote a description of their robots, what they were made of and what they could do. They then uploaded a photo of their robots to an online animation app called ChatterPix, which animates pictures so that they talk. The students drew a mouth on the robot and then recorded themselves in ChatterPix reading the description of their robots using specific vocabulary and grammar structures. As they read, the robot's mouth moved up and down as if the robot was speaking (see Fig. 9.7). What a fun way to practice English!

Fig. 9.7
Monika Bandi's students
presenting robots speaking
using ChatterPix

Spotlight and Reward Effort and Success

Many students are motivated by external rewards. In an online environment you have fewer tangible rewards at your disposal, so you need to be a little more creative in recognizing effort and success. Teachers can award points that go toward a course grade to incentivize student performance. Praise is also helpful to reinforce students' efforts but should be used to reinforce behavior under the students' control. It's important that you praise effort over intelligence, so rather than saying, "Wow, your project was amazing! You are so smart!," it's better to say, "I know how hard you worked on this project, and all of your work really paid off. Your project is amazing!" When you connect student effort to positive results, students are more likely to feel that they have control over their learning and confident that they can succeed if they put in the effort.

Another way to highlight student success is to simulate the classroom bulletin board with a virtual wall where you can post student samples. Teachers at one online high school spotlighted students' exceptional projects on a course page they called a "Wow Wall." This not only rewarded students' efforts but also provided students with peer models. At the same school, administrators entered students who had done all their work into a raffle for gift cards (Borup, Graham, & Drysdale, 2014), helping to motivate students for their hard work.

You can also motivate students by using digital stickers. For instance, Esther Park created digital stickers that she uses repeatedly when giving students feedback. Each sticker contains an animated GIF image of her doing various things such as clapping for students and giving a thumbs-up (Fig. 9.8). Even if students need to redo some work, they still enjoy seeing you in the feedback and are motivated to get a new sticker letting them know they did a good job. Some online programs will automatically reward student effort with points and digital stickers or "badges."

Fig. 9.8
Esther Park's digital stickers to motivate students

Ensure Authenticity and Relevance

Students are usually more motivated when learning activities are authentic and relevant to their lives. In language learning, teaching students isolated language chunks or focusing instruction on grammar exercises is not effective. Language is best learned in context, connected to real-world tasks or activities.

On top of that, activities that mirror authentic communication connected to students' goals for using English outside the classroom will be even more motivating. We can get to the heart of student motivation by connecting to their purpose for learning English. This purpose may connect to the students' ideal L2 self as described by Dörnyei (2014). If you have students who are learning English for instrumental reasons, such as to study abroad, you can help them learn appropriate communication in academic contexts by practicing email correspondence and discussion board participation. You might have students learning English for integrative reasons, such as traveling to various countries around the world and using English as a lingua franca to meet people across cultures. You can find some social media groups for travelers or help your learners search for and read travel reviews to make decisions about where to stay and what to do. Such activities connect directly to how your students value learning English and bring authenticity and relevance to your online instruction.

Odalis Monzon Torres in Peru connects her young learners to real-world content by having them participate in a role-play to discuss why some animals are endangered. To make this activity more authentic and meaningful, she focuses on learning and communicating about endangered animals in Peru (Fig. 9.9). This motivates students to talk about the topic since it reflects a real issue in their country.

Fig. 9.9
Odalis Monzon Torres's students discussing endangered animals in their country

As appropriate, you can also add authenticity by sharing students' work with others beyond the class. For younger students, this could include sharing their work on a website for parents or other members of the school. Adult students could share their work more broadly using social media and other online platforms.

Problem-based learning (see Fig. 9.10) has grown in popularity because it situates learning activities in a real-world scenario that students collaboratively address. The result is often a project that can be shared with others. In fact, there are times when actual members of the community can act as stakeholders.

Fig. 9.10 **The stages of project-based learning**

Norma Constanza in Colombia teaches students of all ages and often centers learning activities on authentic tasks and problem-solving. For example, her students conducted a research project to analyze historical issues important to Colombia. The younger students shared their reflections with others in their school; the older students shared their ideas on social media with parental permission. Encouraging students to examine historical events and communicate their perspectives is an authentic contribution to political discourse. In a larger project, her students researched different aspects of climate change and created videos to share their views with the broader community. This activity allowed students to have a voice on an important global issue, all in English. What a great example for making learning real and relevant (Fig. 9.11)!

Fig. 9.11 **Two of Norma Constanza's students' global warming projects**

You can also add authenticity by having students make connections closer to home. For instance, Vanesha Rhaburn in Belize asked her young learners (and their parents) to record simple videos from home in English. The task was to gather items at home that start with a specific letter and then record a video saying each of the items. Encouraging students to share items from home is a simple way to create interest in using English. It's like a home scavenger hunt, and teachers can motivate students even more by asking which student can find the most items that start with a letter.

English teachers are always finding new ways to motivate their students in language learning. This can be more challenging in online and blended environments, especially if both teacher and students are new to this learning context. However, with these simple strategies, you will start to find out what motivates your learners and build their confidence in language learning online.

After You Read

Think about one of the least motivating lessons you have taught online or facilitated using online applications. Fill out this graphic organizer to help you reflect on your experience with this lesson.

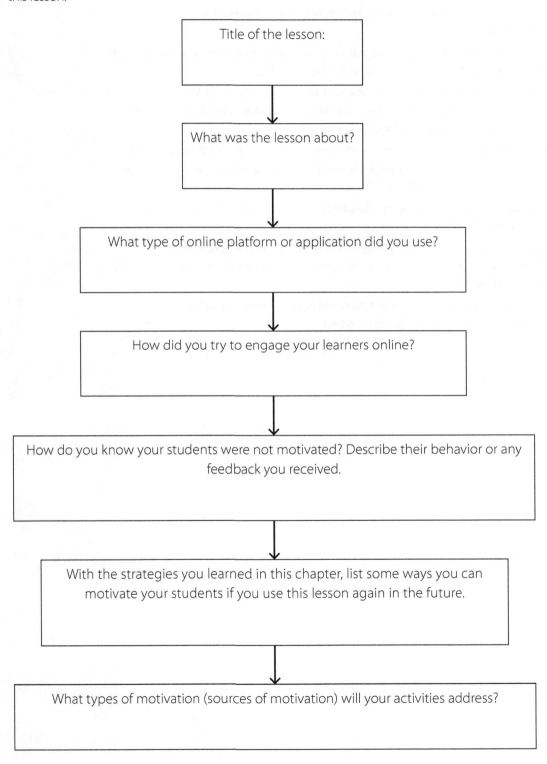

Title of the lesson:

What was the lesson about?

What type of online platform or application did you use?

How did you try to engage your learners online?

How do you know your students were not motivated? Describe their behavior or any feedback you received.

With the strategies you learned in this chapter, list some ways you can motivate your students if you use this lesson again in the future.

What types of motivation (sources of motivation) will your activities address?

References

Bandura, A. (1977). Self-efficacy: Toward a unifying theory of behavioral change. *Psychological Review, 84*(2), 191–215.

Bawa, P. (2016). Retention in online courses: Exploring issues and solutions—A literature review. *SAGE Open, 6*(1). Retrieved from http://journals.sagepub.com/doi/abs/10.1177/2158244015621777

Borup, J., Graham, C. R., & Drysdale, J. S. (2014). The nature of teacher engagement at an online high school. *British Journal of Educational Technology, 45*(5), 793–806.

Dörnyei, Z. (2014). Motivation in second language learning. In M. Celce-Murcia, D. M. Brinton, & M. A. Snow (Eds.), *Teaching English as a second or foreign language* (4th ed., pp. 518–531). National Geographic Learning/Cengage Learning.

Freidhoff, J. R. (2020). *Michigan's K-12 virtual learning effectiveness report, 2018-19*. Michigan Virtual. Retrieved from https://michiganvirtual.org/research/publications/michigans-k-12-virtual-learning-effectiveness-report-2018-19/

Gardner, R. C. (1985). *Social psychology and second language learning: The role of attitudes and motivation*. Edward Arnold.

Losada, M., & Heaphy, E. (2004). The role of positivity and connectivity in the performance of business teams: A nonlinear dynamics model. *American Behavioral Scientist, 47*(6), 740–765. doi: 10.1177/0002764203260208.

Wigfield, A., & Eccles, J. S. (2000). Expectancy-value theory of achievement motivation. *Contemporary Educational Psychology, 25*(1), 68–81.

CHAPTER 10

Empower Students to Personalize Their Learning

The greatest sign of success for a teacher ... is to be able to say,
'The children are now working as if I did not exist.'
- MARIA MONTESSORI

GOALS

By the end of this chapter, you will be able to:

- encourage students to personalize their learning online.
- design and manage personalized learning environments using a learning management system (LMS).
- apply various models of structuring blended learning environments.
- help students manage their own learning.

Girls perform an experiment in a science class at Al-Maarifa Girls Secondary School, Bahrain.

Before You Read

Before you begin reading this chapter, think about how often your students can personalize their learning in your online and blended classes. Indicate how often you allow your students to do each item.

	Often	Sometimes	Rarely	Never
I let students choose or personalize the TIME of day they learn.				
I let students choose or personalize the PLACE where they learn.				
I let students choose or personalize the PACE at which they learn.				
I let students choose or personalize the PATH that they take to learn.				
I give students two or more options of activities to choose from to demonstrate their learning.				
I allow students to make suggestions to me for how they demonstrate their learning.				
I provide students with the opportunity to give me feedback on my instruction and the online classroom environment.				

Introduction

We don't have a one-size-fits-all world. Products seem to come in every size, color, flavor, and style. Internet access gives us seemingly unlimited choices in how we entertain ourselves. Through streaming services, we can watch TV programs, movies, and videos when we want and on the device of our choice. Increasingly, we can get *what* we want *when* we want it.

This level of personalization has clearly benefited our lives, but those benefits have come at a cost. While choice is desirable, "it may also prove unexpectedly demotivating in the end," and counterintuitively, there are times when people are happier and more satisfied when they are given some choice but not unlimited choice (Iyengar & Lepper, 2000, p. 996).

Just as the Internet has allowed us to personalize our purchases and entertainment, teachers can leverage the Internet in ways that allow students to personalize their learning. Choice can have a powerful impact on student engagement. At the same time, too much choice can overwhelm some students, especially those students with low self-regulation skills. In this chapter, we will show you how to design and manage your instruction to encourage students to personalize their learning in both online and blended learning environments.

Personalized Learning

Four Dimensions of Personalized Learning

Personalized learning is often confused with differentiated instruction. However, the two are different. In differentiated instruction, the teacher customizes the learning experience for each student's learning needs and interests, whereas in personalized learning, students are empowered to make choices and take some control over their learning. Specifically, there are four dimensions of personalized learning (Fig. 10.1):

1. **Time** of day that students learn,
2. **Place** where students learn,
3. **Pace** at which students learn, and
4. **Path** that students take to learn and demonstrate that learning.

Fig. 10.1 **The four dimensions of personalized learning (based on Horn & Staker, 2011)**

Students can personalize their learning without technology, but it's easier to do in blended and online learning environments. In fact, personalized learning is such a core of blended learning that it's included in its definition:

> Blended learning is any time a student learns at least in part at a supervised brick-and-mortar location away from home and at least in part through online delivery with some element of student control over time, place, path, and/or pace. (Horn & Staker, 2011, p. 3)

The element of student control in blended learning models needs to be managed wisely by the teacher, because while personalized learning can empower and motivate online and blended students, having too much choice too early is a recipe for frustration and possibly failure. Students—especially younger ones—may lack the maturity and ability to thrive in an environment where they can learn at any time, place, or pace. There are some online courses where students have almost unlimited choice. For some students, this flexibility is liberating, and they are able to complete the course much faster than expected. For other students, such flexibility makes it much harder to maintain adequate progress in their course.

Strategies for Providing Students with Choice in Their Learning Path

As discussed in Chapter 3, content and learning activities that are online already provide students with some choice in their learning time, place, and pace of learning. It can be more challenging to provide students with choice in their learning path, such as what content to study or what project to create, but the following strategies will help.

- **This or That** is an easy way to start providing students with choices without overwhelming them in the process. As the name implies, you provide students with two choices and allow them to pick "this or that." This can be as simple as allowing students to choose between two articles to read or to choose between reading an article and watching a video. Teachers can also allow students to choose between two assignments. For instance, in a lesson about popular dishes from different countries, you could give students a choice to write the recipe for their favorite dish in the correct format or to make a video demonstrating how to make the dish.

- **This, That, or Another** is similar to *This or That* in that you still provide students with two choices but also allow students to propose *another* option. For instance, in the example of giving students a choice to write a recipe or make a video showing how to make their favorite dish, you could allow students to suggest another option. Perhaps students want to give a presentation in real time during your synchronous class instead of recording a video. Or maybe they want to take a recipe that is written in their native language and translate it into English. As long as all options meet the objectives of the lesson or unit, you can be open to providing students with choice.

- **Choice Boards** provide students with a menu of activities or assessments to choose from, commonly organized in a 3×3 table. You can require students to complete a certain number of the options. You can also require students to complete the activity in the center square or the activities in a specific column or row. Figure 10.2 is an example of a board that provides students with choice in how they demonstrate their learning.

- **Passion Projects** (sometimes called Genius Hour) allow students to pick what they want to learn related to the course topic and how they will demonstrate their learning. This allows students to explore and find their passion for the course topic, hence the name "Passion Projects." This doesn't mean that students have total flexibility in what they learn or how they demonstrate that learning. After all, you need to make sure that this project meets the language and learning objectives of the course. It's best if you approve the projects that your students propose or even help students to identify possible projects. You can help students to identify topics using sentence starters such as "I'm interested in knowing . . ." or "I would like to be able to . . . ." You can give students a set amount of time to spend on their project throughout the course. You can also set regular check-in points to ensure that students are progressing in their projects.

Reading Response Choice Board

Learning Objective:

Book Review	Traits	Connections
Create a book review. Include at least 3 reasons why you do or do not recommend the book. Use evidence from the text and do not give away spoilers. Suggested Tools: iMovie, Flipgrid, Slides, WeVideo	List the protagonist and antagonist's internal and external character traits. Include evidence from the text. Suggested Tool: Sheets	Create a Slideshow sharing at least 4 connections from the story. • Text-Text • Text-Self • Text-Movie • Text-World Suggested Tools: Slides
Link	Link	Link
Vocabulary Use the highlighter to select at least 3 unfamiliar words from the digital text. Write each word in a sentence. Suggested Tools: Read and Write for Google extension, Docs, Slides	**Directions** ☐ Complete 3 or more activities. ☐ Use the paint bucket to fill in each completed box. ☐ Paste the link to the completed activity. ☐ Turn in your work to Google Classroom	**Book Trailer** Create a 2 minute book trailer to get other students interested in your book. Suggested Tools: iMovie, WeVideo, Powtoons EDU, Slides with Screencastify
Link		Link
Interview What 5 questions would you ask the main character during an interview? Find a partner to respond. Suggested Tool: Google Forms	**Point of View** Retell the story from the antagonist's point of view. Suggested Tools: Book Creator, Google Slides, Docs, Flipgrid	**Timeline** Create a timeline that includes at least 6 major events from your story. Suggested Tools: Google Drawings, Slides, Jamboard, Seesaw
Link	Link	Link

Fig. 10.2 **Example of a Choice Board**

Gaytri Kandaiah in Malaysia provides an example of how personalized learning can help to motivate students. She explains:

Students in my [online] classroom have the autonomy to choose which language activities (role play, impromptu speech, debate, group discussion, written tasks, etc.) they wish to participate in every week. By allowing them to decide, this has increased my students' participation in the online classroom.

Gaytri uses interactive online communication tools, where she and students can post content using text or video. She has found these especially helpful in providing students with choice and opportunities to share information and encouragement. For instance, when Gaytri taught her students how to express opinions, she allowed them to practice by choosing from a list of topics and making a short video to post online.

Structuring and Managing a Personalized Learning Environment

While it's important to provide students with choice in their learning, you also need to carefully structure and manage the personalized learning environment. Students are less likely to learn in a disorganized learning environment, whether in person or online.

Structuring the Online Environment

Online and blended teachers need to use tools and platforms to provide their students with a structured online learning environment. Commonly teachers accomplish this using a learning management system (LMS) as an online classroom. An LMS provides teachers and students with a single password-protected online environment where students can access learning materials, submit assignments, access grades and feedback, take quizzes and exams, engage in discussions and collaborations with peers, and receive announcements and other communications from their instructor. An LMS also allows the teacher to create learning modules and sequence learning activities, affording students more personalization in their learning time, place, and pace of learning. Figure 10.3 shows an example of learning modules and a sequence of learning activities created in an LMS.

You may also wish to create course content on a website outside of the LMS. For instance, Katie Bruechert, a librarian in the United States, created a website for her course content and learning activities (Fig. 10.4). By creating a website rather than using an LMS, Katie had more control over the organization and layout. The

Module 1: Introduction to Teaching English to Young Learners (TEYL)		
Module 1: Overview		
Module 1: Task 1 - Video Lecture (30 minutes)		
Module 1: Task 2 - Read Articles (2 hours & 30 minutes)		
Module 1: Task 3 - Self-Assessment Quiz (1 hour) Jan 13 | 15 pts		
Module 1: Task 4 - Discussion (1-2 hours) Jan 13 | 10 pts		
Module 1: Task 5 - Assignment: Learning Environment Profile (3-4 hours) Jan 13 | 10 pts		
Module 1: Wrap-up		

Fig. 10.3 **Sample module and sequence of learning activities created in the LMS Canvas**

website also wasn't password-protected, so it was easier for her students and others to access. For those things that needed to be more secure, such as assessment submissions and grades, she used a password-protected LMS that she linked to on her website. Creating a website sounds complicated, but it's not. Unlike in the past when you had to know HTML or another coding language, today you can easily create professional-looking websites with text, images, and videos without any coding knowledge and at no cost.

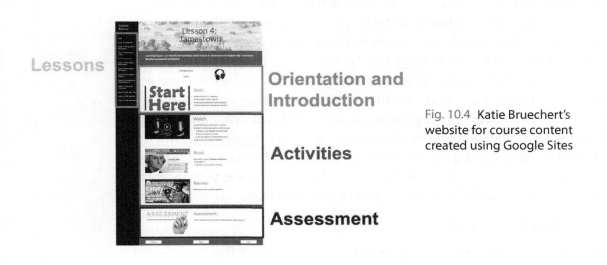

Fig. 10.4 Katie Bruechert's website for course content created using Google Sites

In addition to websites, you can use word-processing documents and presentation slides to create content and learning activities. In the following example, Corey Teitsma, a teacher in the United States, first created content and assignment directions in Google Documents and Google Presentations. He then organized them with other materials and activities such as orientation videos, discussions, and readings in the Google Classroom LMS (Fig. 10.5).

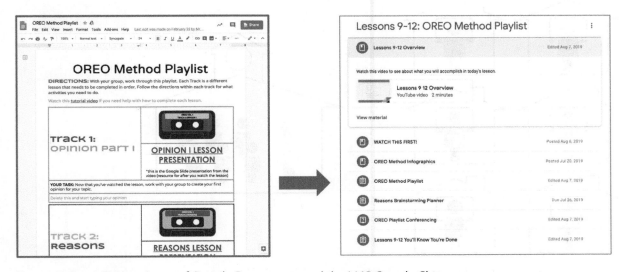

Fig. 10.5 Corey Teitsma's use of Google Documents and the LMS Google Classroom

Structuring the Blended Environment

Blended teachers need to provide students with a structured environment both online and in person. Technology can change how you structure your in-person environment, but teachers and students in different schools have different levels of access to technology. In some schools, every student is given access to a computer, and in some cases, students are even assigned computers to take home. Some schools may provide classrooms with a computer station with a few computers for students to share. Other schools may not have computers for the classroom but instead offer a computer lab where teachers can sign up to take students for certain sessions. Lastly, some schools may only provide their teachers with computers and implement a Bring Your Own Device policy where students can bring technology from home.

Your level of access to technology determines the types of blended learning that you can implement and the level of personalization that students can have in their learning. The Clayton Christensen Institute, a nonprofit, nonpartisan think tank in Boston dedicated to improving the world through Disruptive Innovation, has done extensive work to identify different blended learning models that describe how teachers can structure the blended environment so that students can best personalize their learning and the teacher can best differentiate instruction. We will look at some of these models.

THE FLIPPED CLASSROOM MODEL

The Flipped Classroom model (Fig. 10.6) earned its name because it flips the time and location where learning typically occurs. Traditionally, the teacher introduces new concepts in class and then assigns homework that allows the student to practice the concepts introduced in class. With the Flipped Classroom, students first learn new concepts at home, typically by watching videos provided by the teacher, and then when they are at school, they apply their learning in activities that would have traditionally been homework.

There are several potential benefits to this model compared to the traditional way of assigning homework. For instance, when students are asked to complete assignments

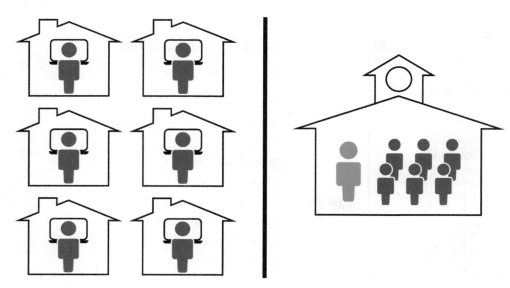

Fig. 10.6 The Flipped Classroom Model

from home, it can frustrate those who struggle because the teacher isn't there to help when they need it most. If students do the "homework" at school, teachers can be there when students are most likely to have questions. Teachers can also use their class time to work with students one-on-one and in small groups. This makes students' time in class more active and collaborative. And for the "homework," students can enjoy having choice in where and at what pace they watch instructional videos. For instance, older students might go to a café, or younger children might be at home sitting on a sofa with their parents. Some students might even meet up with a classmate and learn together. The homework videos allow them to work on learning the new concepts at their own pace, as they can stop or rewind the teacher's video or read texts at a speed that suits them.

And so the Flipped Classroom allows students to personalize the place and time of their learning. However, it doesn't allow them to personalize the path of their learning. Another limitation is that the Flipped Classroom only works when all students have access to an Internet-connected device at home or wherever they want to do their homework. Additionally, many students can't or won't watch or read material at home prior to class for a variety of reasons. Because of these challenges, some teachers prefer the Flex Model.

THE FLEX MODEL

In the Flex Model (Fig. 10.7) most, if not all, of students' learning occurs in the brick-and-mortar classroom with their teacher. Even though students and teachers are in the same room, students' primary instruction and learning activities are done online, largely at their own pace. The teacher's role is to monitor students' learning and focus support where needed. The teacher can also strategically group students and facilitate certain lessons.

Fig. 10.7
The Flex Model

A variation of the Flex Model is when students supplement their in-person courses with an online course and complete that course at their brick-and-mortar school in the presence of an on-site mentor (Fig. 10.8). The on-site mentor doesn't replace the online teacher, as they are not an expert in the course topic. Their job is to help students to "learn how to learn online" and to ensure that students are engaging in their learning activities and progressing in the course. And so while students are taking an "online" course, their experience is actually blended, since they are supported in person by their mentor and online by their teacher.

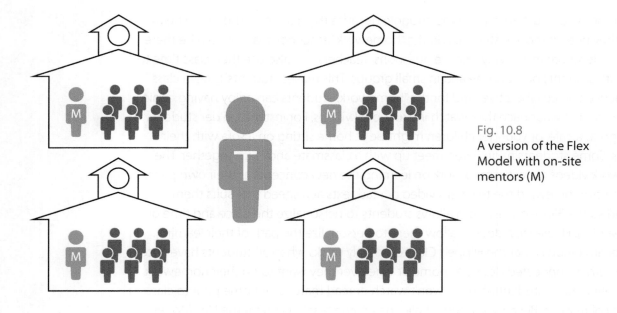

Fig. 10.8
A version of the Flex Model with on-site mentors (M)

THE LAB ROTATION MODEL

In the Lab Rotation Model (Fig. 10.9), the entire class rotates between online and offline activities on a set schedule. Commonly, the offline activities occur in the classroom and the teacher and students move to a computer lab for online learning activities. However, if it is a classroom where each student has access to a computer, the teacher can schedule when the class uses their computers.

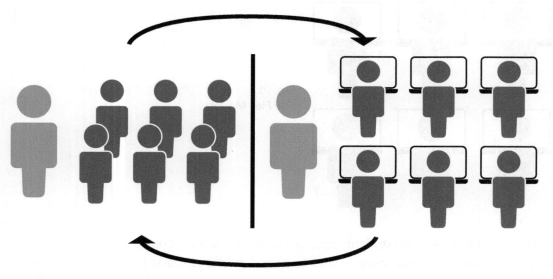

Fig. 10.9 The Lab Rotation Model

THE STATION ROTATION MODEL

In the Station Rotation Model (Fig. 10.10), the teacher creates different learning stations within the classroom that students rotate between. For instance, at one station students may engage in online instruction. At another station, students collaborate and interact with each other. In the third station, the teacher can work with students in small groups, identifying student needs and providing students with targeted support. Throughout the class, the students rotate at timed intervals so that they experience all of the stations.

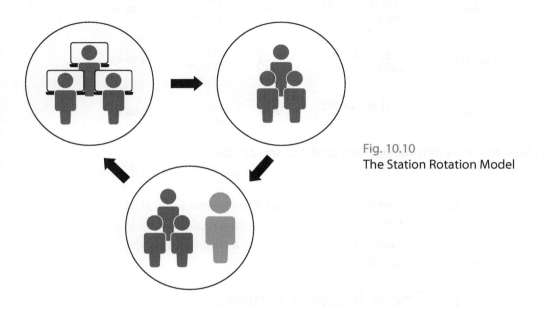

Fig. 10.10
The Station Rotation Model

Helping Students to Manage Their Learning

Once you've created personalized learning activities and structured the learning environment, it's important that you help students to manage their learning in that environment.

Check Students' Digital "Footprints"

In online learning, when you are not physically present, it can be difficult to know what students are doing. In fact, even when you are physically present, students may not be using the technology as you intended. Student submissions are a good indicator of effort and behavior, but that only gives a glimpse into how students are spending their time online. If students haven't submitted work, it's important to reach out to them with encouragement and support. Using your LMS can be a good way of keeping track of your students' digital footprints and providing support when students have not been participating.

Your LMS may allow you to see the last time that students logged on, the time they have spent in the system, and what pages they have accessed in the course (Fig. 10.11). This behavioral data can be especially helpful to recognize when students' efforts are low and when they could use extra encouragement before they fall too far behind.

Name	Login ID	Section	Role	Last Activity	Total Activity
Liz	12340000	ENG 101 Winter 2021 Section 1	Student	Feb 18 at 11:45am	14:18:46
Abdul Rahman	12350000	ENG 101 Winter 2021 Section 1	Student	Feb 17 at 1:49am	24:36:19
Saeed	12360000	ENG 101 Winter 2021 Section 1	Student	Feb 19 at 3:38am	21:39:43
Monika	12370000	ENG 101 Winter 2021 Section 1	Student	Feb 19 at 3:47am	15:05:21

Fig. 10.11 **A sample course in Canvas with last login and total time spent in the course**

You can also track students' progress when you use online collaborative documents that allow you to view the various stages of your students' work. For example, Google Documents' version history saves and timestamps previous versions of a document so you can easily see what was accomplished on specific days.

Provide Office Hours and Check-In Opportunities

It is always a good idea to be accessible to your students, but when you teach online or in a blended situation, you can easily burn out if you feel that you need to be supporting students at all hours of the day. Online "office hours" are a helpful way to support your students while still allowing you to maintain a balanced life. Just as in an in-person setting where students come by your office or classroom for personalized attention, online office hours provide a virtual space where students can easily find you when they need extra help. Perhaps you can set a day and time to be there for students to pop in and talk to you. Or you can have students schedule an appointment to meet you during your virtual office hours. Depending on the number of students, you may even want to require students to schedule times to check in with you. To save time scheduling meeting times, you can create a bookable calendar using an online calendar tool. See Figure 10.12 for an example that shows office hours in 30-minute slots that students can click on and reserve with their instructor.

Seek Student Feedback

You should also encourage students to provide you with feedback on your instruction and course. Hattie's (2009) groundbreaking research found that "the most important feature was the creation of situations in classrooms for the teacher to receive more feedback about their teaching" because it created a "ripple effect back to the student" (p. 12). When you share a classroom with students, it's easy to see how they are feeling or if something isn't working and more direction is needed. However, in an online environment

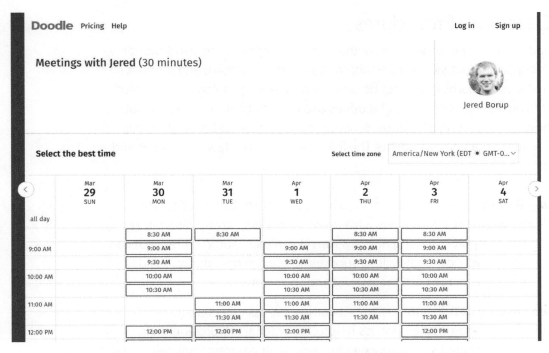

Fig. 10.12 Online calendar Doodle used for bookable 30-minute student–teacher meetings

you need to be more proactive at seeking feedback from students. Mid- and end-of-semester surveys can be helpful checks, but often the feedback is more helpful if it is given in the moment. One strategy to receive more timely feedback from students is to create an open feedback survey that students can always access from your course's navigation sidebar such as the "Fixes and Tips" survey that Jered Borup links to in his graduate courses (Fig. 10.13).

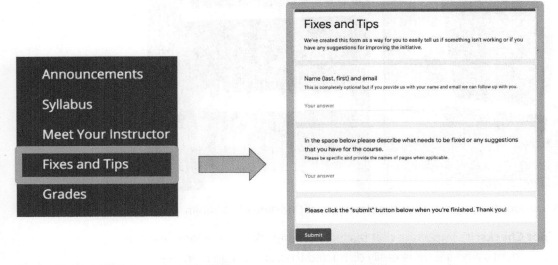

Fig. 10.13 Google Forms survey linked to a course for student feedback at any time

Establish Classroom Procedures

Since blended students spend part or all of their learning time in a brick-and-mortar environment, it's important for teachers to establish classroom procedures and routines so that students can focus on learning and not be distracted. When technology is integrated into students' learning, new procedures and routines also need to be introduced so that students learn how to learn with technology. Younger students need to be taught more procedures and routines than older students. The following are only a few procedures and routines to consider:

- **Recharging Breaks:** Often, electrical outlets are too far from students' desks to have students plug in their computers while they are working. In any case, having students on the computer too long not only runs down their laptop battery but can also leave students with low energy. It's important to build in time during the day when students can recharge both themselves and their laptops.

- **Numbered Parking Lot:** Just as apartment complexes assign residents with a numbered spot in their parking lot, it's helpful for teachers to provide their students with a numbered spot to park and charge their devices. Christine McLaughlin in the United States was provided with a laptop charging cart to use, and she numbered the slots and the corresponding laptops (Fig. 10.14). She can easily keep track of the laptops when each student has their own unique number. Similarly, it can be helpful to give students spots for other materials such as headphones.

Fig. 10.14 **Laptop charging cart from the classroom of Christine McLaughlin**

- **History Spot Checks:** It's important that teachers set on-task expectations. Teachers of younger students, who are more easily distracted than adults, can hold the students accountable by doing random spot checks of their browsing history to deter off-task behavior.

- **No Backs to the Wall:** When students are given flexibility in where they sit, they may naturally want to sit with their back against the wall. However, that makes it difficult for you to easily see what's on their screen, so you may want to consider a no-backs-to-the-wall policy. Christine McLaughlin uses a no-backs-to-the-wall policy (Fig. 10.15) so that the student's laptop screen is easy to see from other parts of the classroom.

Fig. 10.15
Christine McLaughlin models no-backs-to-the-wall policy.

- **Time's Up:** When you need students to stay on schedule, it can be helpful to display a digital countdown so that students can better pace their work.

- **Clam Up:** You probably already use signals for getting your students' attention, and here's one for when your students are working on laptops. When you need them to stop what they are doing and focus on you, you can ask them to "clam up." Students then have to close their laptop like a clamshell so that they can't see their screen (without shutting it down—otherwise, they'd have to start it up again).

- **Hire Students for Your Tech Team:** If you are in the habit of assigning students jobs to help out with classroom management tasks, such as taking attendance, cleaning the board, or passing out papers, you might consider doing the same for jobs related to technology. Since these tasks require a bit more skill or attention, you might consider "hiring" students for these jobs. Rather than assigning students jobs, you can have them apply for the jobs and use it as an opportunity for them to practice English in a job interview. Once they are "hired," you can provide them with some "on-the-job training" so that they more clearly understand how to fulfill their responsibilities. This teaches students responsibility and helps students develop a sense of community and ownership of their learning. Bianca Cahill, a sixth-grade teacher in California, also gives her hired students a lanyard so that other students know to go to them for tech support (Relay, 2016a).

- **One-way Street:** If you are using the Station Rotation model, having students rotate between stations can be a bit chaotic. To avoid having students bumping into each other, it's helpful to establish a one-way street policy so that everyone is rotating in the same direction. If you are teaching younger students, you can break the process down step by step. Caitlin Travaille, a fourth-grade teacher in California, counts off the rotation. When she says "one," students gather their things. When she says "two," students stand by their chairs, and when she says "three," they rotate to their next location (Relay, 2016b).

- **3B4ME:** An important strategy for online learning is to teach students strategies for helping themselves. We want them to become independent learners and not reliant on the teacher to answer every single question, big and small. The "3B4ME" ("Three before me") strategy is useful for teaching in any context, but it can be especially helpful when students are learning online and encounter technology issues. If students are able to resolve their technology issues before asking you for your help, it will free you up to spend more time providing feedback on their learning. Using this strategy, students should do three things before they come to you looking for an answer: play around (experiment) with the tool, search online for a solution, and then ask a friend or parent/family member for help (Fig. 10.16).

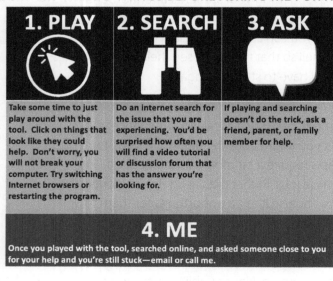

Fig. 10.16 "3B4ME" graphic

Conclusion

Your students will come to your class with different experiences and expectations about online and blended learning. With your guidance and facilitation, your students can enjoy the freedom of personalizing their learning with regard to time, place, pace, and path. It will be important to set up your LMS and other learning applications to support students and help them manage their own learning. Once you establish a structured learning environment that complements your students' readiness to manage their own learning, you will see the benefits of personalized learning for your students. The strategies in this chapter will be a great start!

After You Read

Task 1: Write some ideas for personalizing students' learning time, place, and pace based on what you learned in the chapter.

Learning context	How to personalize student learning	Technology
Online		
Blended		

Task 2: Think about the next lesson you will teach. Think about different kinds of activities or assignments that provide students with choice and are related to your lesson. Write down at least one idea for each type of activity that you learned about in this chapter.

My next lesson (title and/or topic): _____ Lesson objectives: _____	
Type of choice	**Ideas for your next lesson**
This or That	
This, That, or Another	
Choice Board	

References

Borup, J., Graham, C. R., & Drysdale, J. S. (2013). The nature of teacher engagement at an online high school. *British Journal of Educational Technology, 45*(5), 793–806. https://doi.org/10.1111/bjet.12089

Clayton Christensen Institute. (n.d.). What is blended learning? Retrieved from http://www.blendedlearning.org/basics/

Hattie, J. (2009). *Visible learning: A synthesis of over 800 meta-analyses relating to achievement.* Routledge.

Horn, M. B., & Staker, H. (2011). *The rise of K–12 blended learning.* Clayton Christensen Institute.

Iyengar, S. S., & Lepper, M. R. (2000). When choice is demotivating: Can one desire too much of a good thing? *Journal of Personality and Social Psychology, 79*(6), 995–1006.

Relay. (2016a). Green lanyards. Video obtained at https://vimeo.com/185348579

Relay. (2016b). One way streets. Video obtained at https://vimeo.com/185348800

CHAPTER 11

Promote Communication

"Learning another language is not only learning different words for the same things, but learning another way to think about things."
- FLORA LEWIS

An online class led by National Geographic Explorer Joe Grabowski

hangouts.google.com is sharing your screen.   Stop sharing   Hide

Exploring B...

GOALS

By the end of this chapter, you will be able to:

- promote authentic communication, both synchronously and asynchronously.
- manage student interactions by assigning groups and student roles.
- facilitate communication by writing effective prompts, guiding discussions, and encouraging student moderators.
- maximize student engagement by varying online activities.

Before You Read

Task 1: Before you begin reading this chapter, reflect on the ways you encourage your students to interact with each other in English during class time or for your class assignments. Think about your last few lessons and the types of activities you facilitated that encouraged communication among students.

1. How often did your students interact with each other in English during class time?
2. How often did your students interact with each other in English outside of class time?
3. Were the interactions:

   - online, in person, or a combination of online and in person?
   - synchronous or asynchronous?
   - through listening and speaking? Or reading and writing?

Task 2: Now that you have reflected on the ways your students interact with each other in English, think about some of the challenges you face when encouraging interaction among students online. Write down a brief reflection about this.

My challenges encouraging interaction in English in my online learning environment

The Importance of Promoting Authentic Communication in English

In order to prepare our students for communication in English, we should give them plenty of chances to learn and practice real-world interactions. After all, to learn a language, you have to use it! Whether we are teaching students in person, online, or a combination of both, we need to engage our English learners in authentic communication to prepare them for real-life interactions outside of the classroom.

First, let's consider some examples of real-life interactions that your students engage in on a daily basis, whether socially as young people or professionally as working adults. The following are some ways your students may interact with others in real life:

1. having conversations with friends,
2. emailing and texting with friends,
3. posting updates on social media,
4. commenting on others' social media posts,
5. organizing and running a meeting with coworkers, and
6. delivering a presentation and fielding questions.

Notice that these are a combination of in-person and online interactions. This reflects our real lives and the ways we use language in different settings and for different purposes. When teaching English in online and blended learning environments, it's important to consider what types of real-life communication skills your students need for success in English outside of the classroom, both online and in person.

Think about what type of English class you are teaching and your students' needs and interests. If your students are adults taking a business English class, then the interactions you promote in class should reflect interactions in business settings. For example, you could plan lessons around how to write an agenda and organize a meeting or how to make an effective marketing presentation through videoconferencing. If your students are in an intensive English program to prepare them to use English for academic study, your lessons could promote interactions like project work with peers, or etiquette for emailing a professor. Teachers of children and teenagers can encourage interactions that are appropriate for students' ages and interests, such as talking or texting about preferences (like favorite superheroes and video games) or creating and sharing a meme about a lesson topic.

These are just a few examples from different types of classes, but notice how the interactions are online, in person, or a combination of the two. For instance, even when organizing an in-person meeting, your students will need to write an agenda and email it with an invitation to attend the meeting; conduct the meeting; and take meeting minutes, edit those minutes, and email them to attendees after the meeting. Younger learners creating a meme might post it in a private online noticeboard you have created for your class and then comment on each other's memes both online and in person. Some of these activities are synchronous (e.g., talking about preferences and doing a presentation through videoconferencing) and some are asynchronous (e.g., emailing and posting a meme). This mixture of interaction types reflects how we live and communicate in today's world.

Framework for Preparing Student Interactions Online

In order to prepare your lessons in online and blended environments effectively, it will help you to plan out the types of interactions you will facilitate. Consider a framework as shown in Figure 11.1. Even if your class is 100 percent online, your students may have opportunities to interact face-to-face. Or, if your class meets every day in person, your students might interact with each other online asynchronously. We have to promote interactions in ways that make the most sense for our context. In order to set your learners up for success, you can plan your activities with these aspects in mind:

1. **Type of interaction:** Synchronous (happens in real time) or asynchronous (does not happen in real time).
2. **Language skills for interaction:** Receptive (listening, reading) or productive (speaking or writing).
3. **Location of interaction:** Online, in person, or both (blended).
4. **Support for interaction:** Controlled (with language support) or independent (without language support).

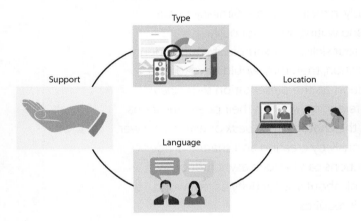

Fig. 11.1 **Framework for preparing student interactions online**

Type of Interaction: Synchronous or Asynchronous

When you plan your activity, you should first decide what type of interaction will be involved. Does the interaction happen synchronously or asynchronously? If your activity reflects an authentic, real-world interaction, then this will likely be predetermined. For example, if the lesson is about meeting someone new and building students' social communication skills by talking about preferences and hobbies, then you should plan for students to do this interaction synchronously through videoconferencing, as building students' conversational language skills in this type of context should ideally happen in real time. However, there are countless examples of authentic asynchronous communication which you can replicate in your activities, for instance, writing a college admissions letter, sending emails in the workplace to a coworker or a boss, posting to social media, or texting with friends and family.

There are also advantages to having students discuss course topics and practice language skills asynchronously even when it's possible to communicate synchronously (online or in person). For instance, whole-class synchronous discussions can be energizing, with rapid back-and-forth exchanges, but only one person can talk at a time. As a result, students frequently have to wait for extended periods of time to make a comment or don't have the opportunity to say anything at all, especially if the discussion is dominated by just a few students who are the most vocal. Additionally, students who are shyer or less confident in their English-language skills can find it difficult to comment in a fast-moving discussion. Asynchronous discussions, for example on an online discussion board, are just as authentic as real-time ones and have the advantage of giving all students equal opportunities to communicate, with time between exchanges to reflect and formulate their responses.

Language Skills for Interaction (Receptive and Productive Skills)

It's also important to plan out what kinds of language skills students will be practicing in your activity. Will it require receptive language skills—listening and reading? Will it require productive language skills—speaking or writing? For example, to practice social or conversational English about preferences and hobbies, your students will practice listening and speaking, either through interaction in a synchronous session or via audio or video messaging apps and tools if learning asynchronously. In the example of professional emails, your students will be practicing reading and writing asynchronously in their own time. Similarly, discussion board activities allow students to practice reading and writing asynchronously.

Some real-world interactions may require all four skills. For example, if your students are preparing and delivering a marketing presentation, then they would have to *read* some information about a product, *write* information on the presentation slide, *speak* when giving the presentation through videoconferencing, *listen* to their peers' questions and give answers, and possibly *read* questions in the chatbox and *speak* or *write* to answer them. Presentations can also be done asynchronously by creating and sharing a video-recorded presentation, and the same peer interactions can happen asynchronously, with peers posting comments and questions. Think about your activity as real-world communication and plan out the language skills it requires.

Location of Interaction (Online, In Person, or Both)

The location of interaction depends in part on the parameters of your specific teaching context. For example, you might be teaching a class 100 percent online or you might meet with your students every day in a brick-and-mortar classroom. In some cases, you might have a blended learning environment where you meet in person with students some days of the week and online on others, and/or students complete learning activities online outside of class. However, this does not necessarily mean that you are limited to these contexts to promote interaction among students. After you have determined what type of authentic interaction you would like your English language learners to engage in, think about the optimum location for this interaction.

For example, you might meet your students in person, but you know that they need some practice expressing their opinions through writing. You could assign an online discussion based on a controversial topic in the news, and they could participate via a discussion board outside of class.

Or, you might teach an online class that only meets once a week through videoconferencing, but you would like to encourage students to interact in between these class sessions. You could assign students a project that requires them to interact and collaborate with each other by email and videoconferencing outside of your class sessions.

Not only do online communication technologies allow your students to interact with each other, but they also allow them to engage with other students around the world—a concept which is not new in itself, since long before there was the Internet, teachers were connecting students internationally by having them exchange written letters. The main drawback to these "pen pals" was that students had to frequently wait weeks or longer to receive replies. With email, pen pals became "e-pals" with much faster exchanges.

More recently, teachers are having students exchange video messages with other students around the world and are also making class-to-class connections using online teacher communities such as Flipgrid's GridPals to find other teachers wishing to do this (Fig. 11.2).

Fig. 11.2 **From paper to GridPals**

While GridPals allows students to communicate using video asynchronously, Mystery Skype gives them the opportunity to communicate with other students synchronously. Ana Živković, a teacher from Serbia, prepared her students to be able to talk about their country and then engaged with a classroom from another part of the world in a Mystery Skype. She and the other teacher connected with each other and scheduled a time when their classes could connect via videoconferencing. The "mystery" is that students in one class don't know where the other class is from, and they take turns asking yes-or-no questions in an attempt to guess where the other class of students is located. In Ana's case, her students in Serbia were thrilled to find out after asking their questions that the mystery class was in the United Kingdom! Then the students in the U.K. got their turn and asked their mystery class questions until they figured out Ana's class was located in Serbia. After students find out where the classroom is located, they share information about their countries and cultures. In Figure 11.3, one of Ana's students is sharing the Serbian flag with students in the U.K. This type of authentic communication shows students how English can be used as a global language with other English-language students.

Fig. 11.3
One of Ana Živković's students in Serbia sharing information about their country with students in the U.K.

Support for Interaction (Controlled or Independent Activities)

Another important aspect to consider when planning communicative activities is the level of support you will provide for the interactions. Depending on your students' language proficiency levels, you may need to appropriately scaffold their use of English. We often distinguish language activities as "controlled" or "independent." Controlled (or guided) activities have plenty of language support to guide learners and "control" the language that is used in the interaction. A controlled practice activity for beginner students is the use of sentence frames. For example, when facilitating an interaction about hobbies, the teacher might give the students these sentence frames to guide their interactions:

Q: What is your favorite hobby?
A: My favorite hobby is _____.
Q: Why do you like _____?
A: I like _____ because _____.

If you decide to have students practice this synchronously as a conversation, you can prepare a slide with the sentence frames and share the screen. Then students can see the sentence frames while practicing the interaction. The teacher can also provide additional support during the synchronous class, such as providing the translation for a word if a student has a special hobby that isn't in the students' vocabulary. An asynchronous controlled activity for practicing this language is allowing students to make a video of this interaction in which they can prepare both speaking parts. For example, a student could record a dialogue in which the student role-plays both parts. To distinguish the two characters, your student could put a hat on to represent the other character or have one wear sunglasses.

Independent (or free) activities are ones that encourage student interaction without specific language support. Students can freely use language to practice their communication skills. Based on the example of a controlled activity, the teacher could take away the sentence frames after students have practiced and give them an opportunity to talk about hobbies and preferences freely.

MOVING FROM CONTROLLED TO INDEPENDENT ACTIVITIES

Even for higher-level students, teachers might provide controlled practice of new grammar structures and vocabulary before providing an independent or free communication activity. For example, in an intensive English class where students are learning academic English, the teacher might prepare students for an oral discussion about their goals by asking them to have a text message exchange with a partner using these questions:

Questions	Answers
1. What is your main goal in life?	My main goal in life is . . .
2. What are your short-term goals?	My short-term goals are . . .
3. What are your long-term goals?	My long-term goals are . . .
4. How will you reach your goals?	I will reach my goals by . . .
5. Who can you get help from to reach your goals?	I think I can get help from . . .

After they practice asking and answering each other's questions by text chat, they can download the chat and practice asking and answering questions out loud to prepare for a big group discussion.

Strategies for Structuring Communication and Collaboration

Structuring an online or blended discussion can be more challenging than a fully in-person discussion, but with some planning, online or blended discussions can be beneficial. The following are some tips for improving discussions in your course and encouraging more authentic communication in English.

The Best of Both Worlds

Synchronous and asynchronous communication each have inherent advantages and disadvantages. Discussions during webinars and in-person classes can be amazing learning opportunities. The short time between comments can make the discussion spontaneous and allow it to go in unexpected directions. These conversations can also include rapid back-and-forths that make it an especially efficient way to learn and problem-solve. The nature of synchronous in-person or video communication allows students and teachers to easily express themselves using facial expressions and voice inflections. As stated earlier, there are also drawbacks to communicating synchronously because there is limited time for students to listen and respond to each other and participation can be unequal. In contrast to synchronous discussions, asynchronous communication can include all students' contributions, and it also affords students extra time to understand others' comments and formulate their own. This flexibility slows down communication, which allows students to practice and to be better prepared for more rapid synchronous discussions. Asynchronous communication also provides teachers with access to all of their students' comments, enabling them to identify those who need the most attention.

Teachers may choose to provide their learners with a blend of synchronous and asynchronous communication activities and may wish to try the "bookend" approach, using synchronous communication to start and end an activity and asynchronous communication in the middle. The bookend approach helps a teacher ensure that students understand difficult concepts (via synchronous communication) before moving to asynchronous communication.

The teacher then finishes the activity synchronously to summarize what was discussed online and answer any remaining questions. Similarly, teachers may require students to start collaborative projects synchronously so that they can create a plan and organize roles before they start to work asynchronously. Students then meet again to finalize their project before submitting it to their teacher.

Think Small

Discussions and collaborations can be best when students are placed in smaller groups to enable equal participation. The ideal group size can vary based on the task, but generally, instructors should "think small" when it comes to groups. For instance, discussion groups with five students are more likely to have higher participation across all group members as compared to groups with 10 students (Fay, Garrod, & Carletta, 2000). When meeting synchronously via videoconferencing, you can quickly create breakout rooms for students to complete tasks in small groups. For asynchronous learning, learning management systems allow teachers to easily place students in discussion board groups where they can work together in small groups.

Assign Student Roles

When teams of students are tasked with collaboratively completing a project or assignment, they can become frustrated when they feel that they are doing more than their fair share. Assigning students roles for collaborative work is one way to help ensure more balanced participation (Fig. 11.4). Roles can change based on the task, but the following are commonly used:

1. **The leader** ensures that the team has a clear direction and each member is engaged in the process.
2. **The timer** keeps track of deadlines and provides the team with reminders so that the team makes adequate progress.
3. **The recorder** takes and shares notes on what is said and the decisions that were made during meetings.
4. **The communicator** keeps the teacher informed of the team's progress and requests support where needed.
5. **The checker** helps to ensure that all of the project or assignment criteria are met.

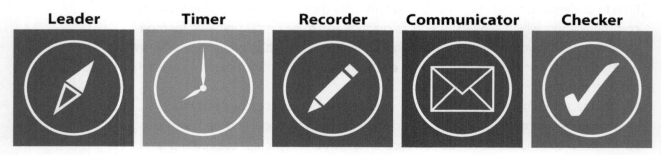

Fig. 11.4 **Roles for group work**

Focus on the Prompt

In an in-person environment, the teacher can spontaneously prompt a discussion by asking questions to launch one. If students don't respond well to the prompt, the teacher can quickly rephrase the question or ask an entirely different question to jump-start the conversation. However, in asynchronous discussions, it's much more difficult to recover from a poor question or prompt. As a result, it's important that you think carefully when creating a prompt.

When creating a discussion board prompt, you should consider the types of communication and thinking that you want students to demonstrate. Prompts can promote (1) convergent thinking, (2) divergent thinking, and (3) evaluative thinking (University of Oregon, n.d.). Discussion prompts for *convergent thinking* commonly start with "why," "how," and "in what ways" with the goal of students working together to refine ideas down to a single solution to a problem. For instance, Esther Park structures some of her convergent thinking activities using an online collaborative whiteboard, Jamboard, where each group member can post comments. She first places her students in groups of up to four students and shares the Jamboard (Fig. 11.5). Each student then records their thinking before and after the discussion, and then as a group they make a single conclusion.

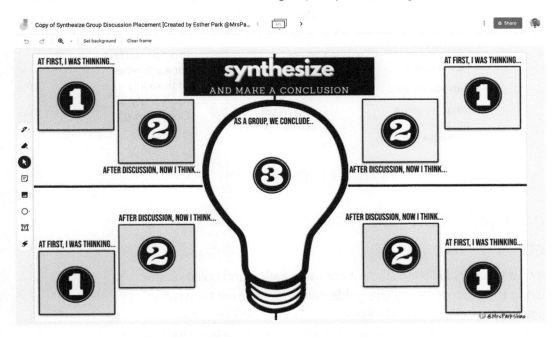

Fig. 11.5 **Esther Park's Jamboard to promote discussion**

In contrast, discussion prompts that promote *divergent thinking* have the goal of identifying many different thoughts and/or experiences. Divergent thinking prompts commonly start with words such as "imagine," "how might," and "if . . . then." Divergent thinking prompts can also help students to relate the activity to their own lives or share previous experiences related to the topic.

Prompts that promote *evaluative thinking* start with words like "judge," "justify," and "defend." Working with peers, students can determine the value or worth of something. In the real world, we are constantly being asked to evaluate products and services, and on social media, we are constantly being bombarded with information and opinions. It's important that students develop the language and the skills to make effective evaluations.

Figure 11.6 shows some sample prompts for the different types of thinking. These sentence or question starters can be helpful when you want to engage students in different types of discussion. Depending on your topic, the language you want students to practice, or your students' language levels, you can write prompts to help them express different types of thinking in English.

Convergent Thinking	Divergent Thinking	Evaluative Thinking
Usually begins with:	Usually begins with:	Usually begins with these words or phrases:
• Why	• Imagine	• Defend
• How	• Suppose	• Judge
• In what ways...	• Predict...	• Justify...
	• If..., then...	• What do you think about...
	• How might...	• What is your opinion about...
	• Can you create...	
	• What are some possible consequences...	

Fig. 11.6
Prompt starters for each type of thinking (University of Oregon, n.d.)

Facilitate Communication

TEACHER "REACTS"

It's important that teachers facilitate student communication and collaboration while not dominating the process, being "the guide on the side" rather than being front and center as "the sage on the stage." Research by Cranney, Wallace, Alexander, and Alfano (2011) found that students' discussion board performance increased when teachers increased the time that they spent in the discussion board, but their performance didn't increase when teachers increased the number of comments that they posted. The lesson learned from this research is that teachers need to monitor what students are discussing but should focus on quality over quantity when it comes to actually posting comments.

There are several times when it's important for teachers to post comments. To help you remember when to comment, you can use the acronym **REACTS** (Fig. 11.7).

1. **R**edirect conversation when students get too far off topic.
2. **E**ncourage student participation.
3. **A**mplify particularly interesting ideas.
4. **C**orrect misconceptions.
5. **T**ease out (instead of giving) answers.
6. **S**how proper language and etiquette.

Fig. 11.7
REACTS

If you remember REACTS, then your students will communicate more with your guidance and modeling to keep them on the right track and interacting successfully.

STUDENT-MODERATED DISCUSSIONS

Assigning students to facilitate discussions on an online discussion board can make discussions more engaging and productive. For example, if you have a unit for your teenage or university students that focuses on giving advice in English, you could assign student moderators to create a discussion prompt based on their interests. They will have a better idea about what kind of advice they want from each other! Before the discussion moderators post their prompt, be sure you have given them plenty of models of discussion prompts so that they will be successful.

A starter–wrapper technique (Hara, Bonk, & Angeli, 2000; Shin, 2016; Shin & Bickel, 2012) is one useful way to have students take charge of the discussion board. For any discussion, one student will be responsible for starting it and another student will be responsible for wrapping it up. The following is an example of how to assign the starter and wrapper roles (Shin, 2016; Shin & Bickel, 2012):

1. **Starter:** This person will start the discussion by identifying an issue related to the topics and readings of the unit. They should post motivating starter questions and/ or pose relevant problems. They will also keep the discussion going by getting participants to share ideas, explore the question(s), and think critically about the topics or problems posed.
2. **Wrapper:** This person will continue the discussion and encourage participants to find solutions to the problems posed by using motivating questions (like the starter). They will integrate the ideas shared by the group and move the discussion forward by highlighting all the new ideas, solutions, and applications constructed by participants. Finally, they will write a wrap-up message that summarizes the main points and issues from the discussion.

For example, if you have set up a class with a weekly module that begins on a Wednesday, you could have the Starter begin the discussion on Thursday and keep it going through Monday. Then the Wrapper would pick up the discussion on Monday and keep it going through Wednesday. This technique encourages students to take on leadership roles in class and be active participants in the online learning community.

It works well when students are assigned a starter and/or wrapper role at the beginning of the semester or a unit of instruction so they have plenty of time to prepare themselves for their moderator role. You should always model the role of starter and wrapper at least once before you assign your students. One way to model both starter and wrapper roles at the same time is to use different fonts or colors to distinguish the two roles. Figure 11.8 shows how the instructor lets the students know which posts are a model of the starter role and which posts are a model of the wrapper role.

Discussion Board Moderators

Email me by August 31, 11:59 PM ET, with your Discussion Board Moderator preferences: **starter** or **wrapper**. Include which week you want to moderate. If you don't have a preference, I will assign you a role.

I will assign the schedule for the Discussion Board starters and wrappers by the end of the first week of class.

Note: I will be the starter and wrapper for the first unit. **My starter posts will be in blue**. **My wrapper posts will be in green**.

Fig. 11.8 Teacher's instructions for assigning discussion board moderators

This is an easy way to distinguish the two types of moderators and give your students a model of both before they take on a role as a discussion moderator. As a model, you can also use the language in the sentence starters for convergent, divergent, and evaluative thinking prompts from Figure 11.6. Sometimes it helps to be explicit and tell moderators directly to use them.

Change Up Activities

There are countless activities that help students to learn through interactions with each other. While there are some benefits to keeping activities relatively consistent throughout the course, you run the risk of students' losing interest unless they change up activities every once in a while. Here are some examples of interactive activities that can help provide variety online:

1. **Reflections and Replies:** Online discussions commonly require students to read or watch something and then share their reflections with their peers. Once they've posted their reflections, they can read and reply to others' comments.

2. **Jigsaw:** Each student researches a different aspect of a topic and then shares what they learned with their group. For instance, if the topic is Olympic sports, each student would research a different sport and then share what they learned with their group.

3. **Round Robins:** In round robins, students read the most recent comment and then build on those thoughts in some way. One type of round robin is a questions and answer (Q&A) chain. In a Q&A chain, students are required to post a question after answering the question that the previous student posted in their comment.

4. **Debates:** Debating different sides of a topic can be an important way to develop a deep understanding of the topic. Students can start the debate by posting their opening statements. Students can then post their rebuttals. At the end of the debate, students can post their closing statements. If you don't have enough time for a full debate, Esther Park recommends having a virtual tug-of-war in an online collaborative document. Figure 11.9 shows how Esther used Google Slides to structure her virtual tug-of-war regarding the statement "Soccer is one sports activity that requires the most cooperation." When students are given permission to edit the slide, they can add comments using text boxes. In this particular activity, Esther had her students use Mote, a free add-on, to actually post audio recordings of their opinions for their peers to listen to.

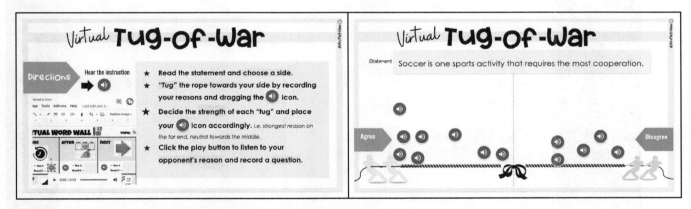

Fig. 11.9 Esther Park's virtual tug-of-war debate using Google Slides and Mote

5. **Peer Reviews:** During work on projects, it can be helpful for students to receive and provide feedback to one another. Teachers can also structure peer reviews using sentence starters and rubrics.

6. **Share Fairs:** Once student projects are complete, share fairs allow students to authentically share their work with others in and out of their class. This can be done in a variety of ways. For example, following a unit on Japanese internment camps in the United States during World War II, each student in Halerin Ferrier's fourth-grade class wrote a letter as if they were actually living in an internment camp. They also created a visual

to represent the feelings that they would have had as a prisoner in the camp. Once students were finished, Halerin helped them to create an interactive presentation as a class so that they could share their letters and art (Figs. 11.10 and 11.11). For this, they used a multimedia sharing tool, VoiceThread, which allows users to upload media (e.g., slides, images, and videos) and post text, audio, or video comments surrounding the uploaded media. In this case, Halerin's students uploaded their art and then posted an audio comment reading their letter. Halerin then shared the presentation with Japanese Americans who actually survived the internment camps when they were children. These survivors and others from the community then posted comments for the students. Halerin recalls, "My students bloomed and excelled during this unit. I was blown away by their work! Seeing them connect and share was all a teacher should hope for."

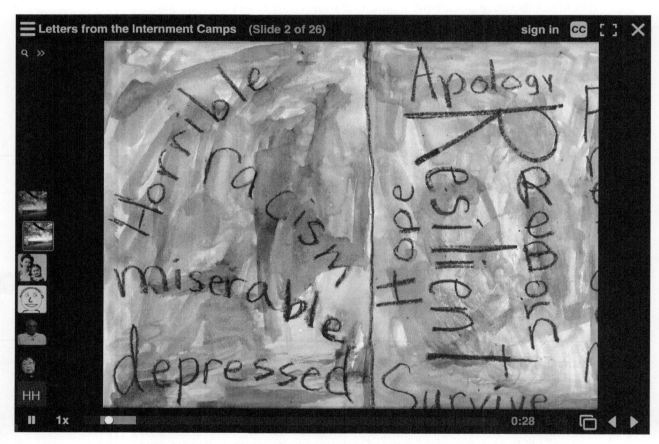

Fig. 11.10 Halerin Ferrier's students' VoiceThread on World War II internment camps

Student letter	Survivor response
March 5, 1943 Dear friend, My brain has turned into a tornado. My stomach feels like it has butterflies in it. Why has this happened? One minute I'm happily making bracelets, in the next minute somebody comes to the door and tells us we need to go to camp because we look like the people who we are at war with. It's so not fair. America doesn't trust us anymore. Today is my first day in camp. Things weren't going so well. If you need to go to the bathroom or take a bath, you won't get much privacy. I can't believe they expect me to live in a place like this. I miss you. Love, Amanda	Amanda, this is Reiko talking and you know what? When you were talking about lack of privacy, you know what I remembered when I was just 8 years old? It was so embarrassing to have to go to the toilet in front of everybody. There were no doors to close. There were no walls on either side of the toilets. There was just toilet after toilet. And it's embarrassing to have to go in front of somebody. Then you have to watch other people go. You know what some of those ladies did? They got very clever. Some ladies got paper bags and they cut out holes for their eyes so people couldn't see who it was sitting on that toilet. Then some ladies did something more. They got cardboard boxes and they sort of opened them up and wrapped it around them like skirts so they could have some privacy while they sat on the toilet. And then Japanese culture stepped in here. Some of the ladies start painting and coloring very nice designs on their little skirts, on these boxes. Then it became competitive to see who could do the best and the most beautiful boxes to put around their toilets. Wasn't that an interesting thing? I thought that you might like to hear that so that was my story to you. Thank you very much for being on this project. Bye.

Fig. 11.11 A student letter from the internment camp project, with a survivor's response

After You Read

Task 1: Think about your students and the types of communication they engage in every day (in any language). What authentic, real-world communications, both in person and online, do your students engage in? What activities can you integrate into your online and blended English-language instruction that mirror these authentic, real-world interactions?

Types of authentic, real-world communication my students engage in every day (in any language)	Activities I can integrate into my lessons that mirror real-world communication
My students use social media to communicate with friends.	Students can create a meme about the lesson topic and post it in our class social media group. They click like and comment on the ones they like the most.

Task 2: Reread your brief reflection from Before You Read Task 2 about your challenges encouraging interaction among students in English. Let's see if you have some new ideas to help you meet those challenges. In the following table, write down the challenges you face in the left column. Then write down some new strategies you have learned in this chapter to encourage interaction in English in your online learning environment.

My challenges encouraging interaction in my online learning environment	Strategies that encourage interaction in my online learning environment

References

Borup, J., West, R. E., & Graham, C. R. (2013). The influence of asynchronous video communication on learner social presence: A narrative analysis of four cases. *Distance Education,* 34(1), 48–63.

Cranney, M., Wallace, L., Alexander, J. L., & Alfano, L. (2011). Instructor's discussion forum effort: Is it worth it? *Journal of Online Learning and Teaching,* 7(3), 337–348.

Fay, N., Garrod, S., & Carletta, J. (2000). Group discussion as interactive dialogue or as serial monologue: The influence of group size. *Psychological Science,* 11(6), 481–486. https://doi.org/10.1111/1467-9280.00292

Hara, N., Bonk, C. J., & Angeli, C. (2000). Content analysis of online discussion in an applied educational psychology course. *Instructional Science,* 28(2), 115–152.

Shin, J. K. (2016). Building a sustainable community of inquiry through online TESOL professional development. In J. A. Crandall & M. A. Christison (Eds.), *Teacher Education and Professional Development in TESOL: Global Perspectives* (pp. 143–160) Routledge (Taylor & Francis).

Shin, J. K., & Bickel, B. (2012). Building an online community of inquiry with student-moderated discussions. In L. England (Ed.), *Online language teacher education: TESOL perspectives* (pp. 102-121). Routledge (Taylor & Francis).

University of Oregon (n.d.). Generating and facilitating engaging and effective online discussions. University of Oregon Teaching Effectiveness Program. Retrieved from https://www.lincoln.edu/sites/default/files/cetl/generating_and_facilitating_engaging_and_effective_online_discussions.pdf

CHAPTER 12
Don't Do It Alone

Alone, we can do so little; together, we can do so much.
- HELEN KELLER

GOALS

By the end of this chapter, you will be able to:

- recognize the importance of student support communities for online academic success.
- explain and apply the Academic Community of Engagement framework.
- form and leverage student support communities.
- build a teacher support community in your local and global communities.

A woman gets a helping hand from another rock climber.

Before You Read

Task 1: Before you begin reading this chapter, think about all the different people you interact with to make sure your students have productive experiences learning in your class. Fill in this word web to show who is a part of your educational community and how you interact.

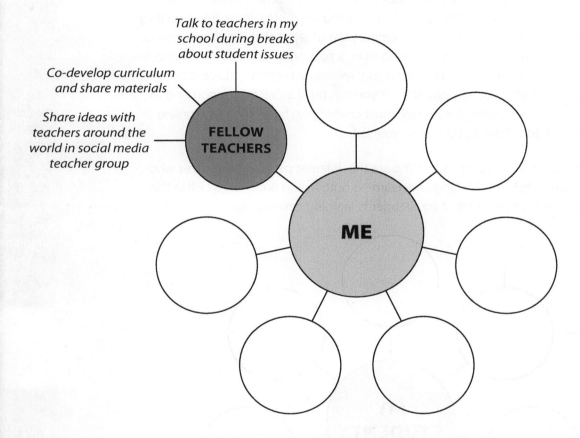

Introduction

Throughout this book, we have focused on how you can impact students' learning in online or blended courses. Undoubtedly, teachers play a critical role in students' learning. At the same time, teachers' efforts alone are not enough for students to reach their full potential. It's important that you don't try to do it alone: remember that you are part of a larger community that is there to support your students. And teachers need support too. Frequently teachers are expected to learn on the job and are more successful when they have a community that they can turn to for support. We usually call this a community of practice (CoP), which is a group of people who share a passion for something they do, like teaching English, and learn how to do it better as they interact regularly (Lave & Wenger, 1991). Later in this chapter, we will look at ways you can build a CoP for support and to further your knowledge. Although you may find it challenging to teach in new online environments, you don't have to do it all by yourself.

Task 2: Think about your students now. Who are the different people in their lives who can positively affect their English-language learning both in and out of class? Fill in this word web and show who is a part of your students' learning community.

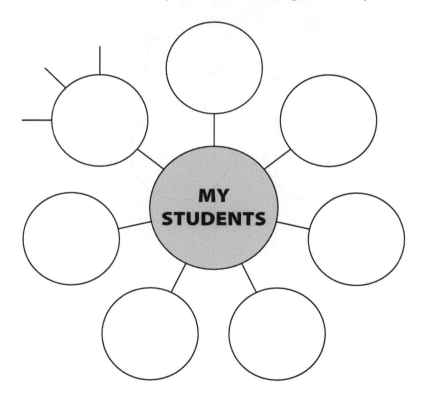

Forming and Leveraging a Student Support Community

Students Need Support from Others to Learn

There are three types of learner engagement that are critical to achieving academic success: emotional, behavioral, and cognitive (Fig. 12.1).

Online and blended students vary widely in their ability to engage emotionally (heart), behaviorally (hand), and cognitively (mind) in learning activities. Each student's

Types of Engagement

Fig. 12.1
The different types of engagement

background and characteristics impact their ability to engage in learning activities. Their ability to engage also changes depending on the topic and/or type of learning activity. For instance, in your English class, it may be harder for some students to engage in a group discussion than in an individual reading activity or vice versa.

When students are struggling to complete online learning activities in English class, there could be a variety of factors affecting their emotional, behavioral, and/or cognitive engagement (Fig. 12.2). For example, their personal environment at home (or wherever they

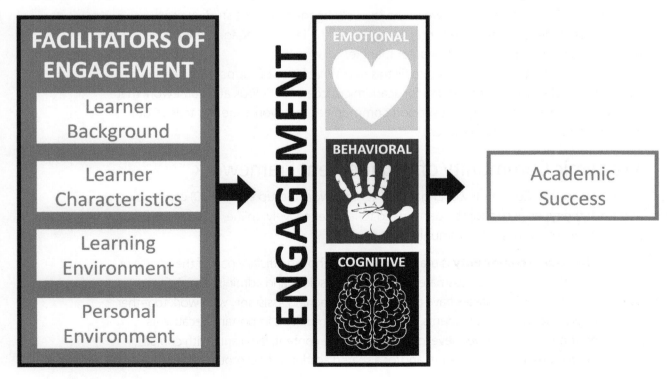

Fig. 12.2 **Types of engagement and their facilitators**

are accessing the course) might either support or limit their ability to engage in learning activities. Likewise, a student's learning environment, which includes teachers, peers, and possibly administrators, can affect their level of engagement. Learners' background and characteristics, such as their motivations for learning English as well as their learning preferences and personalities, can always have an effect on levels of engagement.

In any context, students can independently engage in learning activities. However, their ability to engage *successfully* in learning activities is related to scaffolding or support. This is particularly the case in L2 learning, where students have varying levels of English-language proficiency. The well-known Russian educational psychologist Lev Vygotsky argued that there are three types of tasks: (1) tasks that a student can complete by themselves, (2) tasks that a student can complete with the support of others, and (3) tasks that a student can't complete even with the support of others. Teachers should design language tasks that their students are capable of achieving with support and scaffolding, with the end goal of students using the language independently.

Although we may want our language learners to become more independent and learn how to complete some language tasks individually, for growth to occur you must assign activities that stretch students' abilities. For these activities, students will need support from others. In fact, Vygotsky (1962) argued that what students "can do with the assistance of others might be in some sense even more indicative of their mental development than what they can do alone" (p. 85). While Vygotsky was describing student learning, the same principle can be applied to learner engagement: students' ability to engage emotionally, behaviorally, and cognitively increases when they are provided with support from others.

STUDENT ENGAGEMENT WITHOUT SUPPORT

Figure 12.3 shows the gap between the level of engagement that students can demonstrate independently (the center triangle) and the level of engagement that is necessary for academic success (the outer triangle).

Imagine what students will need to fill this gap. What kinds of support are needed to sustain levels of engagement needed for academic success? Let's look at a framework that can help us conceptualize student support communities that work together to lead our English-language students to success.

Academic Community of Engagement Framework

The Academic Community of Engagement framework (Borup et al., 2020) can help us approach the types of support students need to learn effectively online. This framework identifies two main support communities for students:

1. **The course community** is made up of those who are officially part of the course or school (e.g., teachers, classmates, mentors, counselors, and administrators). Some English-language classes have co-teachers or teaching assistants who work together to provide support to students. The course community is important because its members tend to have a level of expertise in the content, familiarity with course procedures and requirements, and/or a shared academic background.

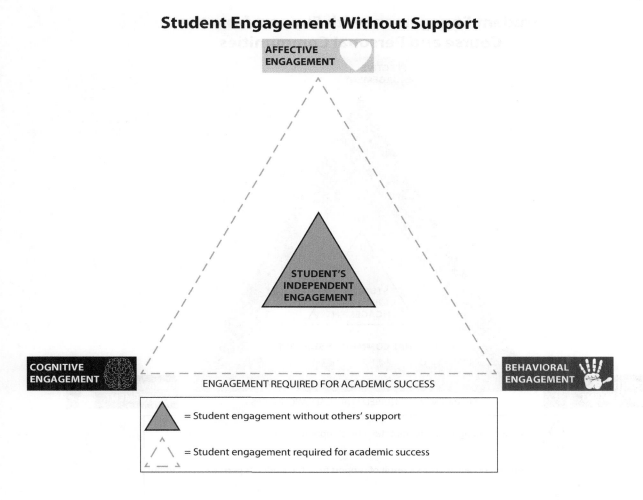

Fig. 12.3 Student engagement without support (adapted from Borup, Graham, West, Archambault, & Spring, 2020)

2. **The personal community** comprises the relationships students have outside of the classroom. Members of the personal community can include parents, siblings, and friends: some have known the student their entire life. The personal community can also include tutors that are hired by the student or their family. The members of the personal community and the influence that they have over the student's learning change depending on the student's maturity and life phase. For instance, parents play a critical role in the learning of children and adolescents, but much less of a role when their children are adults. Important members of adults' personal communities can include spouses or partners, coworkers, friends, and even their children.

Student Engagement with Support from the Course and Personal Communities

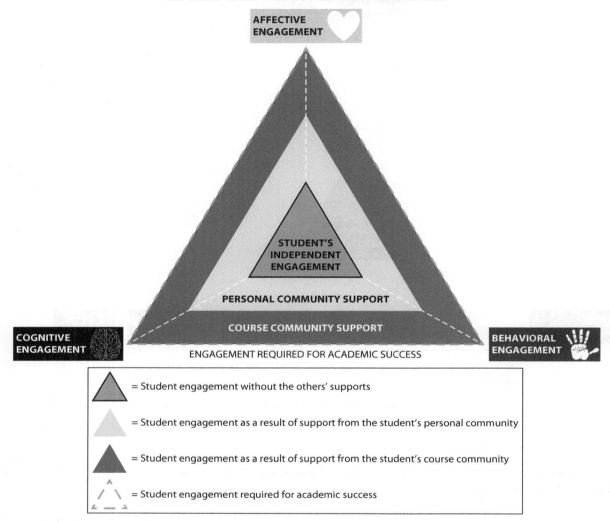

Fig. 12.4 **Student engagement with support from the course and personal communities (adapted from Borup et al., 2020)**

Figure 12.4 shows how the course community and personal community can take students from their level of independent engagement to the level of behavioral, cognitive, and emotional engagement needed for success: in our case, success in English-language learning.

Clearly, teachers play critical roles in their students' success and learning. By following the tips and strategies shared in the previous chapters, teachers can have a greater impact on their students' emotional, behavioral, and cognitive engagement. Teachers can also maximize their efforts when they involve others within the course community. For instance, counselors, advisors, coaches, and facilitators may not know the course content but can develop relationships with the student and support their behavioral and emotional engagement. Additionally, more advanced peers can mentor students both formally and informally.

Even when students are supported by their teacher and other members of the course community, it may not be enough for them to achieve academic success (Figs. 12.3 and 12.4). A teacher and other members of the course community can do everything correctly, but without adequate support from students' personal communities, some students will still fail.

In fully online courses, students' personal communities are especially important. Members of the personal community, such as parents, siblings, or friends, likely share the same physical space as the student, which allows them to support the student in ways that would be impossible for the teacher. Members of the student's personal community can, to an extent, be the online teacher's eyes and ears. Members of younger students' personal communities, like parents or an older sibling, also know students in unique ways, making them especially helpful advocates who can inform the teacher of the student's needs. Older learners might have a study buddy or a conversation partner that can provide support. Table 12.1 highlights several types of support that students' personal communities can provide.

Table 12.1 Possible types of support from students' personal communities

Behavioral engagement	Emotional engagement	Cognitive engagement
<ul><li>Monitoring and encouraging students' progress.</li><li>Orienting students to the online learning environment and expectations.</li><li>Helping students to maintain a regular learning schedule.</li><li>Providing students with a learning space where they can focus on their learning.</li><li>Ensuring that students have the necessary technology and materials.</li><li>Troubleshooting technological issues.</li></ul>	<ul><li>Instilling a sense of excitement for learning English.</li><li>Modeling a value or learning.</li><li>Helping students to feel comfortable communicating with their teacher and others online.</li><li>Assuring students that they can turn to them for help and support.</li></ul>	<ul><li>Learning and practicing with students when they don't have a level of comfort with or expertise in the content.</li><li>Tutoring students in the course content.</li></ul>

FACILITATING SUPPORT FROM STUDENTS' PERSONAL COMMUNITIES

There are several factors that may make it difficult for a student's personal community to provide the support the student needs. For instance, Hoover-Dempsey and Sandler (2005) identified several reasons why parents don't adequately support their students, including:

- lack of time and energy,

- lack of confidence that their efforts will have an impact on student learning,

- perceived lack of knowledge and skills,

- lack of invitations to be involved from the school or teacher,

- a perception that their child doesn't want them involved, and

- a misunderstanding of what role they should play.

These may not be easy obstacles to overcome. However, there are some relatively simple strategies that teachers can use to improve the support that students receive from their personal communities.

- **Take inventory:** At the start of a course, it can be helpful to work with students to take inventory of those in their personal community who could possibly support them in their learning and what specific support roles they can play.

- **Make introductions:** It's helpful for those in students' personal learning communities to feel comfortable communicating with the teacher. For instance, local K–12 schools commonly have "open houses" when parents can visit the school and meet teachers at the beginning of the school year. For classes held online, a teacher can hold a virtual open house using a videoconferencing tool. Additionally, teachers can send their students' personal communities a message introducing themselves, which can include photos and/or video messages.

- **Make specific invitations:** A student's personal community is more likely to support students when its members receive specific invitations to do so. For example, if you teach children or teenagers, you might invite a few parents who can speak English to be guest speakers and talk about their jobs. With adult or university learners, you might invite other students to be conversation partners who can help them practice communicating in English while expanding their personal community. Teachers can also encourage students to extend invitations. And when teachers have the contact information of personal community members, they can encourage them to have conversations with students regarding their needs and the specific ways that they can support students in their learning.

- **Support the supporters:** Members of a student's personal community may be willing to support students but unsure of how exactly to do it. This is especially true when members of the community have never experienced being an online or blended student themselves. In those cases, it's helpful to share strategies and tips for supporting students. It's also important not to overwhelm those in the position to support students with too many strategies and tips at once: a better approach is to share only a few strategies and tips periodically, at the time when they would be the most helpful to students. For instance, teachers and schools commonly can send students' personal communities a regular newsletter that helps to support students in their efforts with specific tips for their current activities. These newsletters could go to parents of younger learners or to conversation partners or tutors of older learners.

- **Provide a window into the course:** It's helpful to keep members of students' personal communities in the loop with what's happening in the course. For instance, teachers may choose to maintain a blog or a group on social media that students' personal community members can choose to follow. Teachers can also regularly send progress reports to parents. At the same time, it's important that teachers don't share anything that would violate student privacy policies or institutional or governmental regulations.

Forming a Teacher Support Community

Support with Technology

Similar to their students, teachers need support from others to be successful. This is especially true if you are new to online or blended teaching because these forms of teaching require different skills and competencies than traditional in-person teaching. One important part of your community will be technological support. Some online and blended programs provide an online technology assistant to provide support for the teacher as well as the students. If students need help navigating the learning management system or can't figure out how to upload a file to submit an assignment, they can contact the online technology assistant. They may be able to do this in their native language, which can alleviate students' frustration with any technology issues.

Having a designated technology assistant can help a teacher focus on their English-language instruction rather than getting caught up in their own or their students' technology issues. Not all teachers will have this level of support, but there may be someone else in their support community, such as a tech-savvy friend (or even teenage child) to help troubleshoot technology issues.

Building a CoP

The fact that you are reading this book shows that you are motivated to improve your online and blended teaching skills. In addition to this book, there are many sources of professional development from publishers, teachers' associations (e.g., TESOL, IATEFL), and governmental and non-governmental educational organizations (e.g., The Online Professional English Network (OPEN) Program, British Council, and Online Learning Consortium). These companies and organizations frequently provide free professional development webinars, blog posts, articles, and virtual events and provide access to their online communities of practice. Social media also allows you to follow and connect with online and blended teachers and other experts. There are many educational social media groups that you can join.

One initiative called Learning Moments 2020 provided an opportunity for teachers around the world to post and share their best moments teaching online with an international community of educators. Many of the Learning Moments teachers have been highlighted in this book. Lorena Rebeca Linares Lemus, a first-grade teacher in Mexico, shared a video in this community with her best moments teaching her young English learners online. Her video ended with a really positive message (Fig. 12.5).

Even motivational messages from a stranger within an international online community—who might be far away geographically—can feel close to home for teachers.

Fig. 12.5 Lorena Rebeca Linares Lemus's video message in Learning Moments 2020

While books, blog and social media posts, and webinars are helpful, nothing replaces the benefits that come from meeting and sharing ideas with other online and blended teachers. Teachers in a brick-and-mortar school can easily have these conversations over lunch or in the hallways. Opportunities for casual conversations with other teachers are less common if you are teaching online. However, online teachers can have frequent communication with each other using email and text messages. Many teachers use messaging apps to communicate with fellow teachers. They might share resources or provide emotional support through humorous posts and memes to keep each other going.

We also recommend scheduling regular times to meet with other teachers at your school using videoconferencing tools. These no-agenda meetings allow for casual conversations and time to discuss challenges and share strategies that work. You can even find a teaching buddy who you can count on for support and vice versa. A fifth-grade blended teacher, Neisha Coutlee, summarized the message of this chapter and the book, "Don't do it alone. Reach out on social media or in your school district to those who are teaching online and blended because there's a lot of people that can guide you to make it to the best experience it can be."

Conclusion

When we think about learning communities, we often think about our classroom or course community. From this perspective, it's up to you and your institution to provide all that your students need to succeed in English-language learning in online and blended environments. However, your students have others in their personal communities who can be instrumental in helping them succeed, and you have others in your teaching support community. There are so many communities of practice both locally and internationally that you can be a part of. Think about teachers who work in your school, school system, or local region as well as teachers across your country or around the world. We are all in this together to find the best ways to engage our students in online and blended environments. Don't do it alone!

After You Read

Task 1: Go back to your word webs from Before You Read. Can you add more to them based on what you read in this chapter? After adding additional people to each word web, review each member of the community and write down how they contribute to your teacher support community and your student support community.

Task 2: Make an action plan for building your teacher support community and reaching out to your student support communities. First, look at your word web and write down a person or people you can collaborate with to help you and your students be successful in online and blended English-language teaching and learning. Then brainstorm how you will engage with them.

Action plan for building support communities	
Who will you engage with?	**How will you engage with them?**
Fellow English teachers	• Start a group on a messenger app and ask my colleagues at school if they want to join it to share ideas. • _____ _____ _____ • _____ _____ _____

References

Borup, J., Graham, C. R., West, R. E., Archambault, L., & Spring, K. J. (2020). Academic Communities of Engagement: An expansive lens for examining support structures in blended and online learning. *Educational Technology Research and Development,* 68(2), 807–832.

Hoover-Dempsey, K. V., & Sandler, H. M. (2005). Final performance report for OERI grant # R305T010673: The social context of parental involvement: A path to enhanced achievement. Presented to Project Monitor, Institute of Education Sciences, U.S. Department of Education, March 22, 2005.

Lave, J., & Wenger, E. (1991). *Situated learning: Legitimate peripheral participation.* Cambridge University Press.

Vygotsky, L. (1962). *Thought and language.* MIT Press.

Cover Shunli Zhao/Moment/Getty Images; **1** Praetorianphoto/E+/Getty Images; **3** Jered Borup; **5** Jered Borup; **8** Jered Borup; **9** (cl) (bc) StartupStockPhotos/122 images/Pixabay, (br) Lukasbieri/146 images/Pixabay; **11** (br) © John shin/Cengage, (bl) 1stGallery/Shutterstock.com, (bc) © Tim Laman /National Geographic Image Collection; **12** (tl) Jered Borup, (bl) iStock.com/Bart Sadowski; **17** © Frans Lanting/National Geographic Image Collection; **25** (c1) © Ken Karp Photography, (c2) Design Pics Inc/Alamy Stock Photo, (c3) 1971yes/iStock/Getty Images, (c4) Joe McBride/Photographer's Choice /Getty Images; **26** (tr) Norbert Eisele-Hein/Look-foto/Getty Images, (tc) Chris Cooper-Smith/Alamy Stock Photo, (tc) DanCardiff/E+/Getty Images, (c) Dsafanda/E+/Getty Images; **27** (tc) © Anastasia Metallinou; **30** Nasa; **33** © Cynthia Evelyn Javes Rojas; **34** © Analys Milano; **35** (tc) Jered Borup, (c) © Khumora Lora Muslimova; **36** © Susana Reyes Melín; **37** © Gotoh Art Museum; **38** (t) Source: Google Map, (b) Source: Google Arts & Culture; **39** Source: Google Map; **40** Source: Google Map; **41** © Leah Carper; **43** Tdub303/E+/Getty Images; **50** © Stacy Du Preez; **51** (tc) Jered Borup, (bc) © Hulun Wang; **52** Kamleshverm/Pixabay; **53** (tl) © Elizabeth Ortiz, (bc) © Fuiyu Gotoh; **54** © Woomee Kim; **55** © Xiao Hu; **58** Cheri Alguire/Shutterstock.com; **61** © Cengage; **62** (tl) (bl) Jered Borup; **64–65** (spread) Jered Borup; **66** Jered Borup; **67** © Cengage; **68** © Christine McLaughlin; **69** © Karen Ours; **70** Jered Borup; **71** (tl) © Corey Teitsma, (bl) Jered Borup; **74** © Ronan Donovan/National Geographic Image collection; **78** © Nathan Williamson/National Geographic Image Collection; **80** Jered Borup; **82** (tl) Jered Borup, (bl) © Chrissy McLaughlin; **83** © Chrissy McLaughlin; **84** © Anastasia Metallinou; **85** (tr) (cr) Jered Borup, (br) © Anastasia Metallinou; **86** (tr) (br) Jered Borup, (cr1) (cr2) GlobalP/iStock/Getty Images, (cr3) © Anastasia Metallinou; **89** Jered Borup; **90–91** (spread) © Chrissy McLaughlin; **90–92** © Chrissy McLaughlin; **95** Vgajic/E+/Getty Images; **99** (tc) © Hamed Hashemian, (b) © Leslie Leisey; **100** © Omid Karden; **101** (t) © Ingrid Nicastro, (bc) © Erika Cano; **103** Jered Borup; **105** (tc) © Katherine Haiduchak, (bl) © Kristin Cady; **106** © Daniel Denisevich; **107** (tc) © Esther Parks, (c) © Virginia Bruno; **108** © Philippe Petit; **109** © Irmak Yildiz; **112** LeoPatrizi/E+/Getty Images; **113** Jered Borup; **114** Jered Borup; **116–118** Jered Borup; **119** (t2) Davies and Starr/Photographer's Choice/Getty Images, (tc) ZSSD/Minden Pictures, (cr1) Adie Bush /Photonica/Getty Images, (cr2) Johann Schumacher/Getty Images, (cr3) Siede Preis/Photodisc /Getty Images, (cr4) Matthew Heinrichs/Thinkstock, (cr5) Zoonar RF/Zoonar/Thinkstock, (cr6) Thinkstock, (cr7) Alistair Berg/DigitalVision/Getty Images, (cr8) Hutch Axilrod/The Image Bank /Getty Images, (cr9) Chris J. Price/Photodisc/Getty Images, (cr10) iStock.com/GomezDavid, (cr11) iStock.com/onepony, (cr12) Nils Smelteris/Thinkstock, (cr13) Njpolice/Dreamstime.com, (bl) Davies and Starr/Photographer's Choice/Getty Images, (br1) (br2) (br3) FirstShot/Alamy Stock Photo, (br4) (br5) Thinkstock, (br6) Siede Preis/Photodisc/Getty Images, (br7) PavelRodimov/iStock/Getty Images, (br8) © Cengage 2019, (br9) Zoonar RF/Zoonar/Thinkstock, (br10) Adyna/iStock/Getty Images, (br11) Njpolice/Dreamstime.com, (br12) iStock.com/onepony, (br13) Nils Smelteris/Thinkstock, (br14) Hutch Axilrod/The Image Bank/Getty Images, (br15) Adie Bush/Photonica/Getty Images, (br16) Chris J. Price/Photodisc/Getty Images, (br17) Alistair Berg/DigitalVision/Getty Images, (br18) Prixel Creative/Shutterstock.com, (br19) iStock.com/GomezDavid; **120** (tr) PublicDomainPictures /Pixabay, (cr1) (cr2) Jered Borup, (cr3) Stevepb/561 images/Pixabay; **121** Jered Borup; **129** © Tristan Savatier; **133** © Monika Bandi; **134** © Ingrid Nicastro; **136** © Zeboniso Murodova; **137** (bl) © Sara Gintert, (br1) © Chrissy McLaughlin, (br2) © Chawanna Chamber, (br3) © Katie Talbot, (br4) © Susan Lemery; **138** © Scarlet Rojas; **139** © Monika Bandi; **140** (tl) © Esther Park, (bc) © Odalis Monzon Torres; **141** (t) Jered Borup, (bc) © Norma Constanza Basto Salas; **145** © Annie Griffiths/Life as Lived; **147** Jered Borup; **150** © Gaytri Kandaiah; **151** (cl) © Katie Bruechert, (b) © Corey Teitsma; **152** Jered Borup; **153** Jered Borup; **154–157** Jered Borup; **158–159** © Christine McLaughlin; **164** © Joe Grabowski; **169** (bl) © Ana Živković; **172** Jered Borup; **173** © Esther Park; **175** Jered Borup; **177** © Esther Park; **178** Halerin Ferrier; **179** © Halerin Ferrier; **182** Anatoliy_Gleb/Shutterstock.com; **185** (cl) (b) Jered Borup; **192** © Lorena Rebeca Linares.